The Power
of
Spiritual
Relationships

The Power of Spiritual Relationships

About the author: Gordon Ferguson is a graduate of Northwestern State University and the Harding School of Theology. With more than fifty years of experience, he has served as an evangelist, elder and teacher. He emphasizes leadership training and teaching. Gordon has also written fifteen books and  many audio/video teaching series. Gordon and his wife, Theresa, live in McKinney, Texas and attend the DFW Church of Christ. For more articles, information, speaking schedules, go to Gordon's website at www.GordonFerguson.org.

ILLUMINATION PUBLISHERS

www.ipibooks.com
6010 Pinecreek Ridge Court
Spring, Texas 77379-2513

Contents

DEDICATION
Wyndham and Jeanie Shaw

This book is dedicated to Wyndham and Jeanie Shaw. I write about them in two of the early chapters of the book, describing Wyndham as my best male friend (since my wife is my best human friend). He, along with his wife, played a huge role in my life and in that of my wife. After suffering from a long, devastating illness, he passed into eternity on November 21, 2019. He left a gaping hole in my heart, in the hearts of his family and in the hearts of hundreds who knew him well. He also left pain in the hearts of thousands who knew him to a lesser degree, even if they only knew of him. He was a deserving hero to disciples of Jesus on all continents of this world. As our hearts heal, the gain we received from him will far outweigh the pain. The world was blessed to have this spiritual giant of a man in it for sixty-seven years, and I thank God for him.

FOREWORD

The Power of Spiritual Relationships

Typically, authors begin a book with some knowledge of the subject they are going to write about, then they perform the appropriate research needed to pen a great book, whether it is fiction or nonfiction. The research for this book by Gordon Ferguson, *The Power of Spiritual Relationships*, took little additional investigation. Instead, it is a book about Gordon's life experiences and the culmination of his insight and perceptions through decades of developing, building, losing and strengthening his relationships.

I first met Gordon in the spring of 1988 when we moved to Boston to worship with the Boston church of Christ. Prior to our meeting, I had heard of him as a preacher and teacher in the mainline Churches of Christ. He and Theresa had moved to Boston a couple of months earlier, after becoming a part of what is now called the International Churches of Christ (ICOC). Although we did not realize it at the time, they were to become our disciplers. Now, with the passing of over thirty years, they have become some of Peggy's and my closest friends.

Our initial friendship held little of note. Gordon and I were both making every effort to learn how to be the best disciples of Jesus we could be, but we had little in common other than that. We did mutually enjoy fishing and golf, but that really was the extent of our similarities. He was born in the South; I was from the Northeast. I was raised in a Russian section of the city by first-generation immigrant parents. He was raised in blue-collar America by a typical American southern family. He had been an accomplished musician and trained preacher. I was an irreligious convert out of the campus ministry and a former collegiate athlete with no musical interest other than hard rock. He was more than fifteen years older than me. The relationship we built, and I believe the reason it has stood the test of time, is because of what we are both trying to do: be the best disciples we can be.

Gordon has a unique capacity to passionately show love and concern. His mother, Violet, gave that gift to him. As he aged, he learned how to love deeply because of his amazing relationship with his wife, Theresa, and from the Holy Spirit as he strove to understand Jesus more deeply. He is looked upon by many as a father, especially by those who have had no father or have had difficulty with their earthly father (me included). If you know Gordon well, it is easy to understand why many of us look to him that way. Along with his knowledge and wisdom, he has an unusual aptitude for providing faith, vulnerability and strength through his humility and passion to serve Jesus.

There is a popular acronym in secular thinking, WYSIWYG (What You See Is What You Get). It is a gift of genuineness and authenticity that serves certain people well. Jesus was the perfect example of that gift. Gordon has that gift. A person gifted with WYSIWYG will always speak the truth in love. A friend of Gordon's never has to guess how he feels or what he is thinking. He not only interacts personally that way, but he also writes with the same loving directness. Some may feel this as "off-putting," especially in our current societal context, but true love expresses itself in truth with humility and a personal willingness to learn and grow. Sometimes topics that Gordon addresses, even in this book, can be quickly dismissed because he is too direct. I guess in many ways Jesus was confronted with the same argument, especially by those who may have taken personal offense at certain of his discourses. I think this is why Gordon's relationships span many cross-cultural barriers. I have personally observed his relational prowess with diverse races and cultural ethnicities as well as across generational differences. Gordon's directness brings all people close to him because they trust his genuine feelings and compassion. He is willing to say what he thinks and is humble enough to learn, grow and repent if his thinking and opinions are off target.

I recently had a quiet time on Matthew 23. Specifically, I noted Jesus' teachings to the masses regarding the religious leaders of the time:

> *Then Jesus said to the crowds and to his disciples, "The teachers of religious law and the Pharisees are the official interpreters of the law of Moses. So practice and obey whatever they tell you, but don't follow their example. For they don't practice what they teach. They crush people with unbearable religious demands and never lift a finger to ease the burden."*
> (Matthew 23:1-4 NLT)

The Power of Spiritual Relationships is not just correct teaching. It is also teaching that comes from a man who has lived through victory, challenge, pain, surrender and humility as a husband, father, son, elder, evangelist, teacher, missionary and friend. Through this book, I encourage you to "practice and obey whatever [he tells] you", but most importantly, follow his example and learn from him as a man who is trying his best to follow God. That is what I have tried to do since I first met him, and I have become a better person because of that effort.

Dave Malutinok
President,
HOPE *worldwide* Ltd.
Atlanta, GA

INTRODUCTION

Life is all about relationships. In time, life itself will teach us that. If we don't learn the lesson when we are younger by heeding God's word, advancing age will eventually make it clear, but by then the learning will have been painful—often very painful. Here is what King Solomon wrote as an old man: "Remember your Creator in the days of your youth, before the days of trouble come and the years approach when you will say, 'I find no pleasure in them'" (Ecclesiastes 12:1). However, he didn't share that pearl of wisdom until he had looked for life in all the wrong places. He tried everything that we might today identify as the great American Dream.

As you read through Ecclesiastes, Solomon traces all the dead-end avenues that he had gone down. He speaks of seeking wisdom and knowledge, amassing great wealth, building great projects, enjoying all the pleasures of life that were available, and finally, having great power and position. He was king, after all, and could have and do anything he chose—which he did. Yet he ultimately deemed it all foolishness and a chasing after the wind. Near the end of his life, he wrote the above passage and shared what we all eventually learn: that a life focused on self and what the world offers ends up empty and without pleasure. He wasted years of his existence and ended up depressed and disillusioned. Finally, he figured out what he had in fact first learned as a young man, that God and relationships are the only things that ultimately matter. Here is his conclusion:

Now all has been heard; here is the conclusion of the matter: Fear God and keep his commandments, for this is the duty of all mankind. For God will bring every deed into judgment, including every hidden thing, whether it is good or evil. (Ecclesiastes 12:13-14)

From a practical standpoint, our lives have been shaped by relationships, starting with our parents, siblings, aunts and uncles, grandparents and a whole host of others. When you think back about Christmases past, you don't think of the gifts; you think of the people that shared those special times with you. What would we give for just one more time around the tree with a departed loved one? Our hearts know that life is about relationships, not all the other things that we all too often allow to occupy our minds and time. In the spiritual realm, the more relationships we have enjoyed that called us higher for God, the richer and more productive our lives have been for him. If our church life is not focused on these types of relationships, we will end up lonesome, empty and unproductive.

The fact that life should be focused on relationships should come as no surprise, since the Bible is all about relationships. The highest relationship known to humankind is that with our Maker. Then come the relationships within our physical family, followed by our relationships in our spiritual family, and ending with our relationships with those whom we need to help become a part of God's family. With age comes the realization that relationships are what life is all about. I am thankful for other things, to be sure, as the Bible informs us that we should be (like good food or a beautiful sunset). But I'm not surprised at age seventy-seven as I write this book that every chapter deals with relationships quite directly.

A disclaimer is in order here. I don't imagine by any means that I am a relationship guru (although I write about some who are). My relationship with my heavenly Father has not been an easy one. Like Jacob of old, I often wrestle with God. Some of those wrestling matches come from my difficulty in consistently seeing him as he is rather than seeing him as I often do in my "down" times.

A part of that traces back to my childhood view, an issue I address in one of the book's chapters. Perhaps the biggest challenge in my walk with God is simply my own selfishness. These realizations cause me to end up grateful for God's amazing patience and love, topics that are definitely addressed in the book. Several chapters address our relationship with God, since that is the most important relationship of all. After having what I believe to be a significant breakthrough in my view of God, I added another chapter just before the book went to press. It brought me a much-needed peace and I pray that it will do the same for you if you have similar struggles in this area.

My relationship with my wife is a delight, but that is much more due to her angelic qualities than to the qualities I bring into the marriage. One chapter is devoted to that reality and blessing. To be totally honest, family relationships overall have been something of a mixed bag for me, since I came to understand many of the important principles about these types of relationships later in life through learning about discipling. My growing knowledge of relationships in God's spiritual family helped me see principles I wish I had known much earlier and applied to relationships in my physical family much sooner. My children, in particular, would have benefitted from it while still in their most formative years. I often say that I am a much better grandfather than a father, and I think my family would say amen to that observation. But on the positive side, their forgiveness for my mistakes as a young parent produces gratitude. It's good to be forgiven by both God and family!

Relationships in God's spiritual family have captured my imagination and my heart. This concept we call discipling drew me into my present family of churches, once known as the Discipling Movement. Prior to that, I knew that something essential was missing from most of my church relationships. I had buddies with whom I fished, hunted and golfed as well as associated with in various ways through spiritual activities. But it wasn't difficult to convince me that discipling—the one-another, each-other relationships described extensively in the New Testament—was the missing ingredient in my church experience. Finding those types of relationships in a church fellowship was like finding a hidden treasure. Those relationships are described repeatedly in the pages of this book as I recount how they found fulfillment in my life. As you read of my experiences, you will become increasingly grateful for your similar experiences and thirsty for more of them.

Finally, relationships with those outside the church that lead them to become members of God's family is an essential part of our purpose on earth. Jesus is serious about our role in the Great Commission. Having a purpose that can affect eternity is a blessing that should motivate us for a lifetime. If we are Christians, we were the aim of someone else's outreach to us, another source of motivation to pay it forward by reaching out to others. Conversion stories are all miracle stories, and our own is the greatest of all to each of us. Several chapters in the book relate directly and indirectly to this area of relationships. One will come at you in a very unexpected way. Another will be the most challenging and potentially controversial in the whole book. Look for them!

Introductions to books are designed to accomplish at least two important goals. One, to give you an idea of what the book is about. Two, to engage your interest enough so that you will follow through and read it in its entirety. My prayer is that this introduction has accomplished these two purposes. May God increase your gratitude level significantly as you read and build your motivation to focus on relationships! Now jump right in and enjoy!

1

Old-School Parents

Listen, my son, to your father's instruction
and do not forsake your mother's teaching.

—Proverbs 1:8

I recall reading a little story that began, "I had the meanest mother in the world." It was written tongue-in-cheek by a grown woman describing her youthful view of her mother. From her adult viewpoint, she highly appreciated what she had once seen as mean treatment at the hands of her mom. Of course, the mother in this case had been strict, but in all the right ways, ways that built character and protected her daughter during the challenging path to maturity. I feel much the same way about my parents.

They were old-school and could hardly be expected to be otherwise. I was born in 1942, and my parents had been through some seriously difficult times growing up themselves. They were born in the 1920s and thus were children when the Great Depression hit America. Times for most American citizens were very tough indeed. Just being able to find consistent food and shelter were challenging tasks for millions. My mother's father had died of a sudden illness when she was but three years old. Her mother was left with four children to raise, ranging in age from eight years down to two

Byrle and Violet Ferguson

months old. Add to that challenge the onset of the Depression five years later, and the stage was set for my mother's horrific childhood years. In the case of both parents, their early life and the environments into which they were born marked them emotionally.

Learning aids for parents available in abundance now were nonexistent when I entered the world. My parents couldn't watch TV shows about parenting or listen to podcasts or watch videos on YouTube or attend parenting workshops. Even if they could have afforded it, written materials about parenting were in short supply, if available at all to the average person. Worse, raised in dysfunctional families and having the same type parents as their contemporaries, they simply didn't have great models of parenting from which to learn. They did the best they knew to do, which was seldom the best from an ideal perspective. They did some damage to me in the process, but the things they got right proved to be invaluable to me, and I'm very thankful.

Focus on the Positive

Regarding the damage done, let me give a word of caution here. Although I had to work through the damaged parts, I refused to let it define who I am. Further, in dealing with it, I grew spiritually, and continue to do so. I remember a woman years ago who was in the same church that I was who decided to deal with parental damage in a much different way. She began seeing a professional counselor and learned that her emotional problems were tied to mistreatment at the hands of her father. Although I'm sure that the counselor tried to help her react otherwise, she learned to love hating her dad. It became her focus. Instead of trying to work through the problems she had, she played the blame game with passion. It basically destroyed her. As you think about your parents or other key authority figures in your life, learn from the negative but focus on the positive. You will end up finding more positive than you see at the outset.

I'll start my story with my dad. He was in my earliest years quite harsh, which wasn't good. But since he raised me to hunt and fish (and later bowl and golf), we spent a lot of time together sharing in our favorite forms of entertainment. I'm glad he made me a part of his world in these ways. It certainly helped offset the relationship challenges. When I got married just after turning twenty-two, he took off his father hat and put on his friend hat. That was a part of the Ferguson family culture, evidently, and a welcome one from my vantage point. After that, he no longer felt responsible for me as a parent, so we just became friends. Quite a quick and remarkable transition, as I look back on it.

Hard Work Pays in Two Ways

The two greatest gifts my dad gave me were perseverance in working hard and a determination to always be truthful. The first was inseparably connected to those summer jobs he set me up with and his refusal to let me out of those arrangements. Just after graduating from the ninth grade, to hear that a whole summer of construction work was facing me was not a welcome message. Since I have already described the details in another chapter ("An Unusual Escape from Racism"), I'll leave it at that. I did not enjoy construction work. It was hard, and some of it was flat-out scary. Think walking on steel beams high over multiple sets of railroad tracks carrying a 4 x 8 sheet of plywood—in the wind. Think carrying brick and buckets of mortar four stories high while walking on a one-foot-wide board at the outer edge of the scaffold. Scary! All in all, I hated the work itself.

On the other hand, I enjoyed making the money. It was so hard to come by that I didn't want to spend it. I became a saver and a planner. When I was a senior in high school, I had one brief conversation with my father about college expenses. I told him that I could save enough to pay for all my college costs, including room and board in a dorm, but would appreciate it if he would provide my clothes and an allowance for spending money. He said that sounded fine, and that is exactly how it played out. When I wanted to get married between my last two semesters, that was on me too. I worked on construction jobs during school breaks and some holiday breaks and saved my money. Through it all, I learned to persevere. I never learned how to quit and simply didn't do it except on a couple of very rare occasions with extenuating circumstances. I am so thankful to my father for the gift of hard work and perseverance.

Truth No Matter What

His second inestimable gift to me was to value truth. He would look me in the eye at key times (when I was about to get in trouble with him) and tell me to tell the truth no matter the consequences. Usually those consequences involved his thick belt applied on my backside! Somehow, he drilled truth-telling into my psyche and heart. Learning the lesson was no easier than the one about perseverance, but it has been worth everything to me. My determination to find and follow biblical truths is a part of that lesson learned. Being truthful on a personal level is wrapped up in the same lesson. Sometimes I don't choose to tell the truth in the best manner, as many will attest, but you are going to get the truth from me, rest assured.

Unshakable Belief in the Bible

This gift from my father is very connected to one of the two greatest gifts my mother gave me. In my early years, Daddy wasn't too much into spiritual things. He grew in that when I as a young adult caught fire spiritually. Mother, on the other hand, was quite into spiritual things as she understood them. Her interpretative skills were undeveloped, but one thing was certain: she believed the Bible to be the inspired word of God by which we would all be judged. She put the fear of God into me, although the desire to sin in my youth often won out over the fear. But I never doubted that the Bible was precisely what she thought it was. As a college student, I tried to become an atheist to escape the guilt of my sin, but simply couldn't do it. I discovered that it takes far more faith to be an atheist than a theist. Atheism is a contradiction of human reason at almost every turn. The point here is that my belief in the Bible, combined with my determination to be a person of truth, put me on my spiritual path once I decided to get on it, and the perseverance aspect has kept me solidly on it ever since.

Characters Welcome!

The second gift from my mother was a rather unusual love of people. That gift had some specifics in it that were simply wonderful. Mom loved people in such a way that they quickly felt like part of the family and often became that. She was a mother to many, so I'm not surprised that I have become a father to many. You will want to make sure you read the chapters in the book about two of my "adopted" daughters. Being a father figure was predictable, based on my mother's example.

Byrle and Violet Ferguson

My friends loved my mother. She had a way about her that made my house a natural gathering place. Plus, she was the best cook I have ever known. She loved cooking and stealing recipes and I loved her doing it, as did my friends!

In addition to her uniquely broad type of family love, she loved characters. I really like that byline of one television network that reads, "Characters Welcome." That could have been my mom's byline. She was definitely a character, and she made me into one. She attracted them. I could literally write a whole book on the real characters to whom she introduced me. Looking back, I don't remember us hanging out with too many ordinary people. Some of that is attributable to our broader dysfunctional family perhaps, but there was some fun in the dysfunction.

As a result of this "gift" (and it was a gift in my opinion), I am a bit weird, but I wouldn't change most of my weirdness. I never feel out of place with any type of person (excepting the fully normal ones—and there aren't many of those). I never feel out of place in many settings. It is all quite intriguing to me. Trying to figure out what makes people tick makes me tick! Think about that one— weird, huh?

Finally, my mother's love included a love for children. I love babies and little kids. They start off so cute and develop into highly entertaining personalities as small children. If you know the right questions to ask, the answers are anything but predictable and are quite entertaining. I saw a little plaque once that said this: "Children are God's verdict that he has not yet given up on the world." I like that. Jesus loved children and said that we must become like them to enter his kingdom. That's a sermon all on its own, right? Children have many qualities that we need and an absence of those that we don't need and thus ought to shed.

Gifts That Lasted

My parents, Byrle and Violet Ferguson, have been gone for quite a few years now. The best of who they were, I believe, can be found in me and my kid sister, Pam. I am a preacher and she is married to one. She and I share so much together as a result of sharing the same two parents. She "gets" me in my weirdness like no one else does. She agrees with my estimation of the good and not-so-good things that we inherited from our parents and, like me, believes that the good far outweighs the bad. While the bad parts definitely left their marks, the spiritual growth produced by trying our best to overcome it, combined with the undeniably good parts, made us who we are. And we are thankful! Thank you, Dad! Thank you, Mom!

Into Heart and Life

1. List and describe the three greatest qualities you gained from your parents.

2. What were the main hurts you suffered at the hands of your parents and how has dealing with them helped you grow spiritually?

3. If you are a parent or hope to become one, what key qualities do you want to pass on to your children?

2

An Angel for a Wife

A wife of noble character who can find?
She is worth far more than rubies.
Her husband has full confidence in her
and lacks nothing of value.
She brings him good, not harm,
all the days of her life.

—Proverbs 31:10-12

Of all things for which I am thankful, besides Jesus, it is for my precious wife, Theresa. She is remarkable in very many ways. She is like an angel to me, calling me higher spiritually by her love and her example. I can't quit thinking about her. I can't quit talking about her. I have managed quite innocently to get other ministers in trouble because of how many times I mention my wife when preaching and teaching. Once after conducting an all-day teaching event, the wife of a ministry friend of mine counted the times I mentioned Theresa and called her husband on the carpet for not coming anywhere close to mentioning her as often in his lessons. Sorry about that, my friend! I just can't help it. And I couldn't help writing a book about our marriage a few years ago, entitled *Fairy Tales Do Come True*. My marriage has been like a fairy tale to me, happy ever after—for fifty-five years now.

Why do I view my wife as something close to an angel? For many reasons, starting with her level of spirituality. We try to close out every day praying together. On occasion, we confess our sins when praying. As I listen to her unload her heart about what she sees as her most serious sins, I am struck with amazement. Oh, to have only that to confess! What she sees as her serious sins would be on my minor sins list, if on my sin list at all.

Although she has fairly serious breathing issues, enough to be diagnosed as having COPD (Chronic Obstructive Pulmonary Disease), she just doesn't miss having morning quiet times. Even when our day starts at the crack of dawn (think catching an early morning flight), she will get up three hours early so she can spend time with God. In weak moments, I have accused her of being legalistic about it. She is utterly unfazed by such accusations, saying calmly that she cannot deal with the day without starting it with God. That's quite convicting, wouldn't you say? She's not an angel, but the closest thing to it I have ever known. Her spirituality is shown in countless ways and is deeper than I can really grasp.

Nagging Not Allowed!

Another way that she is an angel to me is in her Christlike ability to call me higher at my worst moments without being negative and condemning. The book of Proverbs says a lot about wives who nag their husbands. Look at these verses from the Holman Christian Standard Bible version:

> **Proverbs 19:13** – A foolish son is his father's ruin,
> and a wife's nagging is an endless dripping.
>
> **Proverbs 21:9** – Better to live on the corner of a roof
> than to share a house with a nagging wife.
>
> **Proverbs 21:19** – Better to live in a wilderness
> than with a nagging and hot-tempered wife.

My wife is not like the wives described in Proverbs 19 and 21. She is very much like the one described in 1 Peter 3:1-2: "Wives, in the same way submit yourselves to your own husbands so that, if any of them do not believe the word, they may be won over without words by the behavior of their wives, when they see the purity and reverence of your lives." Theresa wins me over time after time by refusing to nag while simply displaying her amazing spiritual character. In the dedication of my book *Romans: The Heart Set Free*, I wrote this about her:

> Theresa is to me grace embodied on a daily basis. She has endured patiently through my earliest years as a worldly pagan and then through many subsequent years as a religious Pharisee. In all these challenges, she continued to love me *unconditionally*. She was gentle in expressing her desires to have a more spiritual husband and father for her children. She almost never nagged, in spite of the frustrations with which she consistently lived. I rarely felt a heavy sense of disappointment or disapproval from her, although I was aware of the areas in my life that she wanted me to change. She demonstrated that rare but godly quality of calling me higher without being down on me.

Spiritual and Sexual

A third way she has been as an angel to me is in her spiritual understanding of the close connection in marriage between spirituality and sexuality. In this area, she is absolutely amazing. In our younger years, I had a very strong sexual drive, more than matched by hers. We have spoken about physical intimacy in countless marriage retreats, and I won't say more here. I have a chapter in Fairy Tales devoted to the topic, so you can read more there if you feel so inclined. Suffice it to say that this part of our lives has been quite a gift. In our older years, that part of marriage is not nearly so important as in our earlier years, but keeping that marriage vow, "forsaking all others, be faithful to her as long as you both shall live" has not been a challenge, because, frankly, I could never imagine anyone being as good in bed as she is. What a blessing she has been in this regard and in so many others!

Marriage and Ministry

A fourth reason for me viewing her as angelic is her love for and capability in ministry. Some wives go into the ministry mainly because of their husband's dream. I understand that decision in churches which have this expectation of wives, as most of the congregations have in my fellowship of churches. I respect wives who put their husband's dreams above their own and appreciate them for it. But that is not an easy road, and it sometimes leads to places which hurt both the husband and the wife. That decidedly has never been the case in our marriage. My wife has been all in for all the ministry adventures upon which we have embarked, and there have been many. In our years of marriage, we have lived in well over thirty different residences in a half dozen states or countries, most of them because of our ministry roles.

Theresa loves the Book of Ruth and had a song in our wedding that used some of Ruth's vow to her mother-in-law, Naomi. One line is, "Whither thou goest, I will go." At the time, Theresa assumed, as did I, that we would live in our hometown all our life. Little did either of us suspect that later, a mutual ministry dream would lead us all over the world. But she was a very willing participant in it all. We have both loved it. Recently someone introduced me before I was to preach and said that he had no idea how many countries I had been to in my years of ministry. After getting up to speak, I repeated what he had said and added that I had no idea either. It has been a lot for sure, all accompanied by a willing wife, happy to be serving and delighted that the Lord would so graciously lead two kids from Louisiana into such adventures as we served him. An amazing life of adventure with an amazing wife who relished it all! How blessed am I!

No Flinching in Spiritual Battles

Finally, another vital part of her sharing in the ministry with me has been her ability to handle the seriously difficult times. We have been through some spiritual battles in the ministry, the likes of which have all but destroyed some couples. My father was a boxer,

Gordon and Teresa Ferguson

streetfighter and barroom brawler as a young man, but changed dramatically later in life. I inherited those qualities in a spiritual sense, and although they were unsavory in the physical realm, they have been invaluable in the spiritual realm. I don't have much of a conflict-avoidance, people-pleasing system as a result. From my earliest beginnings in ministry, I have ended up dealing with numerous difficult situations. I don't seek them out, but they seem to come my way. Imagine being married to someone who frequently ends up being where the buck stops. My little wife has handled that role beautifully.

For one thing, she believes that such is a part of our God-given role. For about a decade, our role included working with young churches in Europe. When challenges came, we were most often the ones catching a plane to deal with them. As kids, we used to watch a TV Western titled *Have Gun, Will Travel.* My wife used to say of us, "Have Sword (Bible), Will Travel," and travel we did. She embraced the opportunities to deal with the challenges, just as I did. We were a team, and we each did the parts we were best at.

Her wise advice to countless distressed women helped calm their storms. It was quite amazing to watch her at work. Her calm, loving spirit had quite the effect. After working with the church in Houston for a couple of years, the leaders presented us with two framed sets of materials based on the Texas Rangers. We were depicted as Texas Spiritual Rangers in the presentations, which now hang on the wall of my home office. Theresa loves all of it, including the battles that were at the time quite daunting.

One way that she managed to deal with the challenges was that she didn't take on my battles. She thought that I was a lightning rod and often a target, but she trusted God to help me work through it. She didn't lose sleep when I did, in other words. After Wyndham Shaw and I wrote *Golden Rule Leadership* and took flak from a few in high places (the common folk loved it), she wanted to order me a T-shirt with a target on the back of it. She kept her sense of humor in the midst of challenges because she had such a strong faith that God would bring us through it and that righteousness would always triumph.

I could add other reasons for calling my wife an angel, but these are enough to help you understand why I feel so blessed. I am thankful for many, many things in life, Christ being at the top of the list; but make no mistake about it, my angel of a wife heads up the list of humans. When the minister pronounced us husband and wife at about 2:30 pm on January 30, 1965, my life was blessed far beyond my understanding and expectations at the time. I thought I had gained a beautiful wife, and I had, but in the process, I gained the world. Thank you, God, and thank you, Theresa!

Into Heart and Life

1. Love in marriage means that we love the whole person, pluses and minuses. List the five things about your mate that you appreciate most. Then share the list with them.

2. After reading this chapter, what are three things that you want to change in yourself? Plan how you will implement each change and commit the plan to your mate.

3. How have challenges outside your marriage affected your marriage? What can you change in your perspective about challenges to protect your marriage going forward?

3

My Best Male Friend and Greatest Hero

A man of many companions may come to ruin,
but there is a friend who sticks closer than a
brother.

—Proverbs 18:24 ESV

That is quite a title, isn't it? You notice I was specific in noting that the subject of this friend and hero designation was a man. That's because my very best friend and very greatest hero is a female, my wife, Theresa. But make no mistake about it, my best male friend and greatest hero is without question Wyndham Thomas Shaw. God put Wyndham in my life at a most significant time, and if he hadn't done that, I shudder to think where my life might have ended up. Other men played key roles in my life at different crossroads, but Wyndham was destined to be the most significant. And as his wife in her oneness with him, Jeanie has been a big part of that.

The term "hero" is defined in various ways. An online search for definitions begins with Lexico's quick and simple definition: "A person who is admired or idealized for courage, outstanding achievements, or noble qualities." That one captures the couple described in this chapter. I both admire and idealize them for all three reasons listed. I know he was, and she is, but human, complete with their frailties, but they come closer to the standards suggested by the term "ideal" than just about any other humans I have known. They are my heroes, providing an upward call for me and for thousands more who knew Wyndham or knew about him and who know Jeanie.

Life is about relationships, and few people excel in all areas of relationships, but my friend and hero did. He was exemplary in his walk with God. He was a marvelous husband, father and grandfather in his family relationships. He was a friend who uniquely made everyone who knew him well feel like his best friend. In his leadership roles in God's family, he was the pristine example of Golden Rule leadership, the title of a book that he coauthored with me. I have never known a man who was so excellent in all areas of relationships. Because of that, combined with my love for him, I cannot write another book on relationships without having him in it, not surprisingly as the subject of two chapters.

A Great Man Gone Home

Wyndham died on November 21, 2019 at the age of sixty-seven, ten years my junior. Because of what he meant to me, I started a new phase of my grieving process that had begun several years earlier when he experienced the onset of MSA (multiple systems atrophy), a terrible disease. Since I work through difficult emotions best by writing, I began writing about Wyndham and our relationship almost immediately upon hearing of his passing. I wrote three Facebook posts, followed by a piece that was used in his Celebration of Life printed program, then I wrote the material I used in his eulogy. Finally, I wrote these two chapters dedicated to Wyndham and his beloved wife, Jeanie, as they and their family deserve to have as much of his life described in print as possible. With that in mind, here are my deepest heartfelt words about him, written with heavy heart yet a happy-for-him heart soon after his departure into the destination of all who love Christ and are called for his purpose.

Aah yes, heroes. So thankful for heroes. On November 21, 2019, my best friend died. My most effective way of processing grief it to put it into writing. I felt compelled to write three posts for my Facebook account after finding out about his death—the first on the evening of his passing and the next two the following day. This story about two of my greatest heroes came straight from the heart—a burdened heart, but a thankful heart. Here are those posts, with the photos that accompanied them.

Facebook Post 1 – Golden Rule Leader

Wyndham Shaw, one of God's most spiritual men and one of God's finest leaders, went home today. We served together for many years and built the greatest friendship I've ever had. I have one sibling, a sister (a dear sister), but Wyndham was the brother I never had. He was the friend who stuck closer than a brother (Proverbs 18:24). We laughed together and we cried together. We traveled the world together. We shared some of the greatest challenges of ministry together and shared some of its greatest joys together. He accepted me, warts and all, and talked me off the ledge more times than I care to remember.

We coauthored a book together entitled *Golden Rule Leadership.* He was the best example of a Golden Rule leader I have ever known. I was under his leadership and alongside his leadership for years, and never one time did I observe him being anything other than the gold standard of leadership. He modeled what we wrote about.

A number of people who understand our relationship have offered me condolences. They know what he was in my life. What many don't know is the role he played in my wife's life. Of all the leaders we ever knew and worked with, male or female, he was her safest place. His influence in her heart and life was profound. He changed us and our marriage and our ministry in ways that only God fully knows.

The kingdom of God on earth lost a unique hero today, and the kingdom of God in heaven gained one. Learning to live in this world without him is going to be a challenge for his family, and his family was a big one—all blood relatives, whether family blood or the blood of Christ, or both. Right now, the world seems pretty lonesome without him. But it is a far, far better one because he graced it with his presence for sixty-seven years. I'm glad you are home now, my brother. I'll see you sooner than later.

Facebook Post 2 – Jeanie, Another Hero

The photo pictures three of my greatest all-time heroes. My wife is one of them. Our dear departed brother Wyndham is another.

The woman by his side is the third. Today much of our focus is on Wyndham due to the pain in our hearts at his transition into the next world. But Jeanie is very much on my heart today as well. As she and I texted back and forth late last night, I said this to her: "No wife in history has ever done a better job of loving her man to his end. Truly amazing. No husband has ever been more loved or better loved. An example for the ages. You are my hero!"

In the early stages of Wyndham's disease, Jeanie didn't want to talk about the reality of death. I thought she was in denial, and I suppose she was, understandably. Her attitude was that she would love and enjoy each day that God gave them together and not worry about tomorrow. You can hardly argue with that from a biblical perspective (Matthew 6:34). She was all smiles and laughter every time I was around them (and there were many times in the past few years). Wyndham was pretty much the same, amazingly. They indeed laughed at the days to come (Proverbs 31:25) and drank deeply from the cup of life on a daily basis. It was flat-out incredible to behold.

In the past few months, Wyndham could hardly get out any words that could be understood. But Tuesday, according to Jeanie, he quite clearly said two things to her—that he was going to die and that he loved her. From that point, she begged God to be kind to him and to their family, and he was. She said that Wyndham went downhill quickly and passed super quickly. He was not in pain and passed peacefully.

A giver to the end, Wyndham donated his brain for the research of MSA (Multiple Systems Atrophy), the debilitating disease that took his body. God now has his soul, the real part of who he was, the man we all knew and loved. I asked Jeanie's permission to post this, and her reply was that she doesn't hold back much these days. I'm glad. She shouldn't. Others need to know her and her story at this challenging time. Her children will handle this bittersweet time just like she is, for she is yet with them and clearly in them. May God comfort and bless you all. You have certainly blessed all of us, and continue to do so.

Facebook Post 3 – This Was Us, as Fellow Elders

As a writer, writing is perhaps my most effective way of working through grief. Last night I wrote a post designed to honor Wyndham. I needed to write it, and he deserved all I said and far more. This morning I wrote a post designed to honor Jeanie. Again, I needed to write it and she deserved all I said and much more. This final post of the day I also needed to write, but wrote simply to explain a relationship between two men—a relationship that was forged at the deepest levels by serving as elders together during some of the most challenging years we ever faced. Facing them together made us what God evidently designed us to be in church leadership. Thank you for giving me the opportunity of sharing this part of our story.

Of all the photos I have of Wyndham and me, the one above is by far the most poignant. It catches us in a pose that would have been typical of us hundreds of times. We were at a wedding, a very happy occasion, but in discussion about some challenge involving the church. I can tell just by looking. As fellow elders, we dealt with serious church issues almost on a daily basis, or so it seems in looking back. We talked on the phone with each other pretty much daily, usually more than once. My wife said we were joined at the hip. I think he and I made a great team as elders, kinda with the good cop/bad cop motif. If you know us, you can guess which part each of us played. I have many other photos that I enjoy looking at more, but none that captures the quintessential Gordon-and-Wyndham-as-elders look quite like this one. It leaves me with a paradoxical mixture of emotions at the close of this day, the day after he left us. As the currently popular TV show title puts it, "This is us."

Into Heart and Life

1. List the top ten people who have influenced your life the most for good and what their main contributions to your life were.

2. List the qualities of what you think make a person a "best" friend.

3. What would help make you a best friend to more people?

4

A Loving Tribute to a Beautiful Life

When Jesus saw Nathanael approaching, he said of him, "Here is a true Israelite, in whom there is nothing false."

—John 1:47, NIV1984

As indicated in the previous chapter, all that has been said about Wyndham Shaw needs to be put into writing and all that has been written needs to be put into print. Besides the three Facebook posts I wrote, Jeanie asked me to write a brief article describing his life for the memorial program. That program was printed, but oddly, it was sent somewhere in Kentucky by mistake and didn't make it to Boston in time for the memorial. Thankfully, Jeanie put the draft of it on her Facebook page, and I'm including it as a part of this chapter. Following this will be the eulogy I delivered at the memorial. These two pieces, along with the three in the previous chapter from Facebook posts, contain my best efforts to describe a man who cannot be described in words alone. But with the help of God's Spirit, what I and others wrote will help you see as big a picture of him as possible. When you do, you will be called higher by his example. That's a promise.

Celebration of Life Program

Upon hearing of Wyndham's passing, one of his longtime ministry friends simply said, "He was a spiritual man among boys." The statement resounded with me, for it summed up a life that went well beyond the oft-used phrase of a life well lived. His life was more than that by a wide margin. He was like Nathanael, a man in whom there was no deceit (John 2:47). He was like Barnabas, whose very name meant "son of encouragement."

In Loving Memory

WYNDHAM SHAW
August 13, 1952 - November 21, 2019

Wyndham was a relationship guru. He excelled in every area of relationships possible, beginning with God and then his fellow humans. As a husband, he enjoyed with his wife of forty-five years a fairy tale come true. As a father, his children arise to call him blessed (Proverbs 31:28) for they have been so blessed by him. As a grandfather, being surrounded by his grandchildren lit his face up with pure joy and being in his presence was their favorite place, to the very end.

Family was far broader than blood relatives, for the blood of Jesus shared gave him a family of thousands. He was admired, respected, sought after and loved deeply by those on all continents. He was a shepherd par excellence, serving as an elder for decades, overseeing the flock of God collectively with great wisdom and feeding the sheep individually with great love.

For males and females of all ages and stages, he was the ultimate safe place, the safe harbor in the storms of life. No matter your emotional state when you came to him, you left with peace and reassurance that life's challenges would be met by God.

The world lost a hero when Wyndham left it, but the impact of his life will live on through all who knew him, loved him and were loved by him. He was indeed a spiritual man among boys in many ways, but one whose life called us higher and will continue to do so. Like Abel of old, by faith he still speaks (Hebrews 11:4).

The Eulogy

My task and privilege today is to give the eulogy. The word "eulogy" comes from a Greek word that means good words or true words. Of course, words can sound good without being true. I have heard eulogies that illustrated the point that many people appear to improve in death—they suddenly become better people. Wyndham does not need to be embellished in death, for his life speaks for itself. If anyone was ever the real deal, it was Wyndham Thomas Shaw.

When I first heard of Wyndham's passing, I thought of two people in the Bible. The first was Nathanael, introduced in John 1:47 with these words: "When Jesus saw Nathanael approaching, he said of him, 'Here is a true Israelite, in whom there is nothing false.'" Jesus was describing his spirituality from God's vantage point. Like Nathanael, Wyndham was a follower of God in whom there was nothing false before his God. In my lifetime, I have been blessed to know a few Nathanaels, but only a few, Wyndham of course being one of them.

The other person I thought of was this one described in Acts 11:24: "He was a good man, full of the Holy Spirit and faith, and a great number of people were brought to the Lord." His very name meant "son of encouragement." That was Wyndham—a good man, a spiritual man, a faithful man, an evangelizer and an encourager. No man encouraged me as much as did Wyndham, many times in many places.

Like Barnabas, he excelled as a leader in the church. He and I coauthored a book entitled *Golden Rule Leadership.* The hours we spent together planning, praying and writing were a highlight of my life. I think we both contributed some very good content, but Wyndham was the best example of a Golden Rule leader I ever knew. As I served under his leadership in the beginning and alongside it for many years, not once did I observe him being anything other than a Golden Rule leader. In my experience, he was in a class by himself in that regard.

A Shocking First Morning

Our relationship began in a pretty unique way. Theresa and I moved to Boston thirty-two years ago this month, arriving on December 30, 1987. We were picked up at the airport by Wyndham and Jeanie in the middle of a blizzard. We hardly knew them, but it didn't take long for us to get acquainted in great depth. A few days after moving into Bedford, we went to their house for our first discipling time together. Wyndham was thirty-five years old and I was forty-five, and he was feeling a little intimidated about discipling us, for several reasons, including the age difference.

After the kids were ushered off to school, Wyndham tried to break the ice by casually asking, "So how are you guys doing today?" I said, "Do you really want to know?" which brought a puzzled look to his face. He said a bit tenuously, "Well, yeah." Let me preface the next part by saying that I don't often do transitions well, and the transition into Boston was my absolute worst ever. But in my determination to be totally honest and vulnerable, I said, "I would like to choke this little woman right now!" (referring to my sweet wife). I would give at least a thousand dollars for a photo of the look on his face at that moment. It was a combination of absolute shock and absolute relief! The intimidation left, for now he knew what to do with us, and he and Jeanie did it. We got with them for hours at a time, days on end, and it resulted in changing our marriage and each of our lives in profound ways.

Looking back at it, I marvel at the wisdom Wyndham had at an early age. It was simply an amazing spiritual gift from the Holy Spirit. Proverbs 15:33 sums it up pretty well in these words: "The fear of the Lord teaches a man wisdom, and humility comes before honor." Wyndham's wisdom changed our marriage and our lives. Wyndham became my wife, Theresa's, greatest hero. He was the male leadership authority figure who restored her trust in authority figures. He was her safe place. In her words, he gave her back her voice of who she really was and who she was intended to be. I'm most thankful for Jeanie's blog about Wyndham's wisdom and her plan to write a book about that wisdom. We need it all in print to keep learning from Wyndham.

A Friend Without Limitations

From that entry point forward, our lives were kept together through our ministry responsibilities the entire sixteen years that we were in Boston. He and I served in ministry together—pretty much constantly most of those years as fellow elders. We did manage to hunt and fish and play golf and Hearts on occasion and had lots of fun, but mostly we worked hard in the church together, literally all over the world. I recently posted a picture on Facebook of us hunting pheasants together. His golden retriever in the photo was named Jordan. All day long as we hunted, Wyndham was yelling commands to his dog, but calling him Gordon and in turn calling me Jordan. It was a fun day and a funny day—and Wyndham laughed all day about the repeated mix-ups with our names.

We had a fishing trip for the ages just before I left Boston, one I think God gave us because leaving each other was really, really difficult for both of us. The next morning after the fishing trip, we each picked up the  phone at almost the same time to call the other and ask if we had dreamed that trip or if it were real. It was that off-the-charts surreal, another little gift from God to good friends.

I often say that Wyndham was the brother I never had and the best friend of my life. But many who knew Wyndham would say that he was their best friend. And most of those would say they thought they were Wyndham's best friend—and in a real sense they would be right. Wyndham had an amazing ability to focus on people when he was with them, making them feel that they were the most important person in his life at the time, uniquely viewed and loved by him. He made people feel special because to him, they were special. Worldly thinking tells us that we can only love a few people at a time in deep ways. Spiritual thinking tells us that becoming like God enables us to love more and more people, more and more deeply. Wyndham was the classic example of the latter, and we were the blessed recipients of God's love through him.

Once we moved away from Boston, I returned many times, on some occasions just to get time with Wyndham and have him talk me off the ledge. No one could do it quite like him. As his health took its toll, my heart broke to see him suffering, and it also broke because I was losing my most trusted mentor and advisor and friend. He was that for me and for many besides me. He had a laser-like focus on each person he was trying to help, and he had a gift to help that was amazingly effective.

Family at the Forefront

That focus was at its height in his family. He loved each of you in unique ways. He studied you, and when he talked about you, his knowledge of you and what made you tick was as sharp as a razor. He and Jeanie had a beautiful marriage for forty-five years. He had deep, meaningful relationships with each of you four children, each relationship tailor made to fit your characters and personalities and meet your needs.

His pinnacle of human relationships came when Emma led the way with the arrival of grandchildren—eight of you, the delight of his life, the medicine that could bring pure joy to his face no matter his pain. His relationship with each of you grandchildren had that same uniqueness that was characteristic of his other relationships. You weren't just a grandkid among grandkids; you were a special person all your own, understood and loved deeply by your Papa. He delighted in each of you, and you lived in his heart daily.

Wyndham and Jeanie handled his illness beautifully. At first I thought they were both living in denial, as many do in similar circumstances, but they weren't. They were just determined to live each day to the fullest extent and not worry about tomorrow. That is, after all, what Jesus said to do in Matthew 6:34. Several times, I talked with Wyndham about death and various aspects of what I call the "endgame." He wasn't afraid to die, and he only cried a few times when talking about it—both when talking about family. He was concerned about Jeanie and some of what she was already facing without him and would face after his death. I assured him that Jeanie and I were great friends and would remain so no matter what—and we will. A host of others will do the same for her.

I also wondered if Jeanie's theological studies and writing were an escape for her, but figured out that they weren't. She did it with Wyndham's blessing and much of it in his presence at his bedside. To me, that has been an unexpected bonus that has blessed her and blessed others like me. We have shared many theological discussions, and she has definitely had a very positive influence on my thinking and studies in the past several years, just as Wyndham did in previous years. That will for sure continue between us. I loved Wyndham as an individual and I love Jeanie as an individual, as does my wife.

When I asked Wyndham the last time if he wanted to die to get out of his suffering, he said no. I wanted to know the details of that answer, and for him it was simple. He said he wanted to live to see all his grandchildren baptized into Christ. I asked how old the youngest one was, and he said two. At that point, I commended him for his concerns and desires, but suggested he was going to have to observe it from a different vantage point. But his ultimate concern was clearly for the spiritual salvation of his family.

What Would Wyndham Say Today?

I believe that salvation is his ultimate concern for each of you today. His prayers have been that in his death, souls would be affected for eternity. We are all going to be the subject of a service like this one someday. None of us is going to escape this odd thing we call death. We will all stand before God and be judged. As a preacher of the gospel, I can never leave my speaking post at a memorial without urging you to deal with your life spiritually, whatever your need and wherever you are with God right now. Personally, I will leave today determined to be more for God than I am now. That is what Wyndham is asking of each of us. The impact of his life was great; may the impact of his death be great as well, and let it start with you, and with me, today. I close with these inspired words from Paul in 2 Corinthians 5:6–10:

> Therefore we are always confident and know that as long as we are at home in the body we are away from the Lord. For we live by faith, not by sight. We are confident, I say, and would prefer to be away from the body and at home with the Lord. So we make it our goal to please him, whether we are at home in the body or away from it. For we must all appear before the judgment seat of Christ, so that each of us may receive what is due us for the things done while in the body, whether good or bad.

May God bless you to be ready for that day!

Into Heart and Life

1. If you were blessed to know Wyndham personally, take the time to write out your own description of him and why he was so special.

2. If today were your last day on earth, what would you want people to say about you after you were gone?

3. What do you need to change to make it possible for people to remember you like that when you are gone?

5

Another Kind of Adoption:
The Story Continues

"Truly I tell you," Jesus replied, "no one who has left home or brothers or sisters or mother or father or children or fields for me and the gospel will fail to receive a hundred times as much in this present age: homes, brothers, sisters, mothers, children and fields—along with persecutions—and in the age to come eternal life."

—Mark 10:29-30

A chapter entitled, "Another Kind of Adoption," was originally written for inclusion in my book *The Power of Gratitude.* In this present book, I added a similar heart-touching chapter involving another of my adopted spiritual daughters, but felt compelled to update my original chapter and include it here. It's just too good to leave out, as you will see. Much has happened in Kelly Flores' life in the two decades since the events described in that original chapter took place. By way of review, I met Kelly, the star of the story, in July 1998 and less than a year later wrote the older chapter. Kelly was twenty-four years old and single back then; she is now forty-five and married with three children.

The Kelly of Today

Kelly is one amazing young woman, who has now earned her doctorate, taught at the university level and served as dean of three different schools within a university. Now she has her dream job in the corporate world, with a position designed to drive the culture, learning and leadership development efforts for the company with a focus on helping employees pursue a purposeful and meaningful life—not just at work, but in all areas of their lives. Although it is a secular company, she gets to incorporate biblical principles without people necessarily knowing it! Talent like hers does not go unnoticed.

When she and her husband, Kye, decided to start a family, she had her heart set on having twins. Then on a biblical tour of Rome, she decided that she wanted those twins to have their genesis in Rome. In spite of the fact that twins do not run in either her family or Kye's, she indeed conceived twin boys in that ancient city, one of whom is named Roman. He and his twin are now fourteen and their adopted brother, Micah, is eleven. Mind you, we are talking about a woman who has been basically deaf since she was a toddler. That's why it takes words like "amazing" to begin to describe her adequately. With her determination, not much can stop her.

For example, Micah came to the Flores family in a most unusual way. He was born to a relative whose drug and alcohol abuse was excessive. As a result, he was in the NICU for fifty-two days. The mother knew that she couldn't take care of the child but wanted him adopted by a relative, which ended up being Kelly and Kye. They had to go through three levels of paperwork and processes and appeared to be blocked by Washington State, their state of residence, because they believed in spanking (in the early ages) for disobedience, defiance and deceit. As is often the case, such discipline was viewed as child abuse, and the adoption was declined.

Kelly appealed to her caseworker's boss, who held the same position, and again to the boss's boss—who also declined. Finally, she got the state involved where Micah was born, sought an advocate from a local Christian adoption agency, and took it to the top dog in the state social services office. After getting bombarded with calls and emails, he relented and finally approved the adoption. Kelly reminds me of the persistent widow who never gave up pursuing justice. In her mind, Micah was destined to be their son, and no one was going to stop them from bringing him home.

The Kelly I First Met

But let's run the clock and the story back to that fateful meeting in July 1998. As stated in the original chapter, Kelly invited herself to Boston for a visit. She wrote on the card she sent me that she knew I was a busy man, but still had to eat, and so asked if she at least could have a meal with me. Talk about being starved for the love of a dad! I wept when I read the card. (I'm weeping now.) So I wrote her back and said, "Just come up and spend a weekend with us," which she soon did. I set her up on a date with a good young man from MIT, and the four of us went up to the North Side (all Italian) for dinner and hanging-out time.

Going back to the car after dinner, Theresa was walking and talking with Kelly's date, and I was talking with Kelly. She was looking at me with lights in her eyes, like a kid in a candy store, or as if she had somehow entered into a fairy tale. I told her something like this: "Kelly, whatever love you are feeling from me now (and I hope she was feeling all that was there), multiply it several million times, and you will start to get the picture of how much God loves you." You may recall from *The Power of Gratitude* that she shared in a communion message that she could see God as a Creator or a Judge, but not as a Father. It was some weekend, as you can imagine.

She came back a second time with her sister, hoping we could influence her; and on that trip, I think we spoke at a singles' service and shared "our" story. We've come a long way together since then. She came a third time to introduce us to Kye, to whom she was engaged or about to become engaged. Our next time together was at their wedding in Savannah. She told me that since I was her dad, she wanted the dad who raised her from birth to walk

her only halfway down the aisle, and she wanted me to take her from there, and then perform the wedding. She also wanted Theresa to share some thoughts for them in the ceremony—all of which we did. It was a beautiful day in a beautiful setting. As I was waiting in the garden where the wedding was to be held, someone came for me and said Kelly wanted to see me upstairs in the bride's room. She, the bridesmaids and her mom were all fully dressed and ready, but as I entered the room, "Butterfly Kisses" started playing and Kelly came over to me for a father-daughter dance in front of that small but special audience.

Her Biological Father

That girl is so far down in my heart she couldn't find her way out if she wanted to (and, of course, she would never want to). But to me, here is perhaps the biggest shocker of all. Several years after our relationship began, her biological father (who had rejected her earlier because of her not being "normal") got in touch with her and wanted to get together with her, to which she agreed. He expressed regret about not being there for her when she was growing up and wanted to have a relationship with her now. She told him that she was fine with having an adult relationship with him, but that she couldn't go back to being a little girl again and make up for all of those missed years. Then she added the kicker. She said, "Gary, as I said, I'm happy to have an adult relationship with you, but to be honest, I don't need an emotional relationship with you as a dad. I have that with Gordon."

Knowing the longing that adopted kids and others in similar situations to Kelly's have to connect with their biological parents, this one blew me away—totally! I still find it almost unbelievable that I could be the chosen one for such an exalted role. Kelly is as much a daughter to me as anyone could possibly be, bloodlines notwithstanding. She is probably more like me in character and personality than anyone I know, which can only be one of those "God things."

The Continuing Story

Through the years we have been able to spend special times together in different settings, often punctuated by those long dad-and-daughter talks at Starbucks (her favorite coffee place, being a Seattle resident!). We have shared our story in a number of church settings, touching the hearts of those who understand kingdom relationships and what God designed them to be. Thankfully, Kye is always willing to keep the kids when she spends time with us, because he understands the importance of her being with her adopted dad. Whatever may have been missing from Kelly's childhood, she and Kye have included it and far more in their own children's lives.

The "far more" consists of some very unusual experiences for their family. They downsized to an RV for two years so that they could expose the boys to other cultural settings, traveling to many states in the US. They were also blessed to go on the HOPE *worldwide* Volunteer Corps to the Philippines in 2017 and to New Zealand in 2018; and in 2020 they are set to do the same in Alaska. They have built friendships with people all over the globe, and their boys are experiencing the world through different lenses. As a businesswoman, Kelly amazingly excels. As a mother, she is almost beyond description.

So those are the highlights of the continuing story. Pretty good ones, wouldn't you say? Sadly, there have been long periods when I haven't stayed in touch with Kelly very well. I recall writing her once (probably more than once) and apologizing for being a poor dad to her by not keeping up with her better. (That has been one of my weaknesses in the past with loved ones.) In reply to my apology, Kelly said, "Dad, you were there for me when I needed you most. We're good." I don't deserve that kind of love, but it has helped me repent—with her and others.

And so the story continues with Kelly, as Jesus' perspective about his church being true family continues to be fulfilled in our relationship. When my own memorial service occurs, she will be one of the speakers for it, rest assured. The bond between us, established by the providence of God, will take us into eternity together.

Into Heart and Life

1. What in this chapter inspired you the most? What convicted you the most? Why in both cases?

2. Who in your life would you really like to spend more time with in order to deepen your relationship with them? Make a plan and carry it out.

3. How can you encourage more disciples to seek out these types of spiritual family relationships and deepen them? Please commit to setting an example yourself and helping others do the same.

6

Another Adoption of Another Kind

Then Jesus' mother and brothers arrived. Standing outside, they sent someone in to call him. A crowd was sitting around him, and they told him, "Your mother and brothers are outside looking for you."

"Who are my mother and my brothers?" he asked.

Then he looked at those seated in a circle around him and said, "Here are my mother and my brothers! Whoever does God's will is my brother and sister and mother."

—Mark 3:31-35

After Kelly Flores and I exchanged some Facebook posts on Father's Day 2018, I thought of another of my adopted daughters who had texted me quite a message that day also. Michelle Garrett, now residing in Colorado with her family, moved to Phoenix in 2005 when we were on staff there. I was leading the ministry region into which she and her husband, John, moved.

A Beginning Based on Honesty

They came from the San Diego church at a time when most of the congregations in our movement of churches were going through some challenges. Leaders were not easily trusted, both because of mistakes we had made and because of something similar to a mob mentality that had invaded the thinking of not a few church members. Suffice it to say that it was not an easy period for leaders or for those whom we were trying to lead. With time and God, most of us worked through it all and grew from it.

This gives you some background for my first meeting with Michelle. She and her family attended our service one Sunday when I was preaching. After the lesson, Michelle came up to introduce herself and inform me that they had moved into Phoenix and into our ministry region. When I gave her my name, she said simply, "Yes, I've heard of you," to which I replied, "Well, what did you hear, good or bad?" I was attempting to be lighthearted, but she was having none of it. She said quickly, "Some of both." I continued, "Well, what do you think?" She replied very seriously and honestly, "I don't know yet; I'll let you know when I know more about who you really are."

Wow—pretty interesting introduction! But I appreciated both the honesty and the bluntness. That is my *modus operandi* and I appreciate it in others. That's probably why I loved living in the Northeast for sixteen years. The people there are nothing if not blunt and often even what has been called brutally honest. I far prefer that to the kind of deceptive communication described in Psalm 55:21—"His talk is smooth as butter, yet war is in his heart; his words are more soothing than oil, yet they are drawn swords." The concept of discipling (by whatever term) has long appealed to me, and my need for honesty in both speaking and being spoken to is at the heart of it. Proverbs 27:5–6 puts it well in these words: "Better is open rebuke than hidden love. Wounds from a friend can be trusted, but an enemy multiplies kisses."

Honesty in All Directions

At any rate, I was immediately drawn to Michelle and quickly grew to love her hubby, John, as well. Some weeks or perhaps a couple of months after they joined us, she came up to me after

The Garrett Family

a sermon with tears rolling down her cheeks. She looked at me very intently through those tears and said simply, "Thank you for being you." That was one of the most touching compliments I have ever received. I get emotional every time I think about it, including right now. From that moment, our father-daughter relationship started to grow, and it has continued to deepen. She writes (texts) me pretty often and tells me ways in which our relationship makes her feel special. In so doing, she always makes me feel very loved and very special as well.

Our relationship has been forged by her very direct communication with me on any subject, perhaps especially the difficult ones. Last year I wrote an article about the women's role (*gender inclusion* is my favored term now). I introduced it on my Facebook pages (personal and teaching ministry pages), and her response to it included a reference to another very serious discussion we had early on after she and her family moved to Phoenix. It shows the nature of deep relationships and what it takes to build them. Here is her Facebook response to that article.

What I have always loved about Gordon as long as I have known him is that he speaks to make God shine, not himself. He will often tell you, "Any good in me is because of Him."

Early on in my relationship with Gordon we came to a tough subject in marriage about purity and sin and openness with our spouse. We both were at very different ends of how we approached this topic. I heard his thoughts about it and he mine. We came to no agreement that day. However, a few days later in a discipling time with him and Theresa he shared how he had to go back, wrestle with God and talk to his wife and how they would communicate going forward about sexual purity. I had never felt so validated about the intensity of this subject in my heart. I had been dismissed by others for years prior.

I only share this as an example of humility at how Gordon teaches and preaches. Papa, your legacy of grace and truth and how you fight to make Jesus the center of all you do and say brings such security and hope as we strive to leave our own children a legacy of faith. Thank you for always speaking on such hard subjects in a way that honors Christ above all. I love you!

Michelle's point in the discussion to which she referred was about spouses confessing their temptations, struggles and failures to each other in the area of sexual purity. Prior to that discussion, I held to the standard view that men only confessed to other men and not to their wives. (In some cases, the wife might prefer that, and if so, fine.) Michelle argued strongly that since the husband and wife were one, they were also one in their challenges with sexual purity and had to help each other. Of course, you cannot help what you do not know needs help. Hence the need for openness with each other. Her fervent convictions on the topic persuaded me and caused me to begin sharing my temptations and struggles in this area with Theresa.

A Happy Father's Day

Here is her note to me on Father's Day 2018.

> Happy Father's Day!! For years of my discipleship, I wrestled with God as Father. With some professional help and a whole lot of God being patient the last couple of years, I've been able to settle into his wings and not just be okay but be proud that my dad is God Almighty. Throughout my years, even in my pre-disciple days, I see how God placed certain men in my life to father me, to show me more of Him. Some were for only seasons of life, and some will forever be near if I call. Thank you for taking your calling from God to be a Papa to many and yet make each of us fatherless girls feel closer to God. You and I are so similar in spirit, backgrounds and personalities that it makes me giggle at God. I love you, Happy Father's Day Papa!
>
> —Michelle

Once again in my life, Mark 3:31–35 and 10:29–30 have been beautifully fulfilled. It's a good day to be a father in the complete spiritual sense of that word. I know that all of us need surrogate fathers and mothers spiritually, even if we have good parents. In the two biblical passages just noted, Jesus himself makes the point quite clearly. My sense is that people read about my relationships with Kelly and Michelle and wish for something similar with older people whom they know. Yet they don't claim those relationships that are there to be claimed.

Learning from John the Apostle

I think of John the apostle, who described himself as the "disciple whom Jesus loved." He mentions this description of himself frequently enough in his gospel to indicate that this was his reputation among his fellow disciples. Do you really think that Jesus loved him more than he loved the other apostles? I think that Jesus loved all of them (as he loves all of us) more than we humans can grasp. John just capitalized on what he knew was there to be taken hold of and enjoyed. That's what Kelly and Michelle have done. It is what you can do with those in your life, and it is what Jesus wants you to do because he knows that you need it. Use the example of my two daughters to follow through with what your heart yearns for! That is why these two chapters are in the book.

A Footnote from Michelle

After sending the chapter to Michelle for her input and approval, she sent back a response that needs to be included. Essentially, she said that from her experience, relationships like she has with me are not as available for claiming as hers was with me. Listen to her in the following:

> I say this all because claiming is a good word and I believe many want to claim such relationships, but in a sense the workers are few and there are not enough older couples, empty nesters and such who are reaching back to us in the trenches of raising teens, parenting adult children, not enough of us marrieds reaching back to singles, not enough singles reaching back to campus or teens. I know many times I have felt exhausted and discouraged, literally begging people for insight into my life stage. This truly is where gratitude comes in as I've had to place myself in God's arms first, dig deeply into his word and pray for the right person at the right time, all the while making sure I stayed grateful by reaching back and not leaving someone else feeling as I have felt in my different seasons of life. So, I don't know if you wanted my 50 cents worth but there it is! I love you. I love this concept. I love us and our story! I pray that many, many more get to claim the relationships that help them see the face and heart of God more clearly!

Into Heart and Life

1. Write to three people in your life who are among your closest "blood of Christ" family members and express your love and appreciation to them.

2. Have you found other disciples open to deepening relationships who are either a good deal older than you (parent figures) or younger than you (who could become your spiritual children)? Have you initiated with those both younger and older than you? Will you?

3. What do you need to imitate in the life of the Apostle John that would enhance your relationships with those whom you cherish most?

7

An Unusual Escape from Racism

Now let the fear of the LORD be on you. Judge carefully, for with the LORD our God there is no injustice or partiality or bribery.

-2 Chronicles 19:7

For those with much knowledge of recent history in the United States, telling you that I grew up in the '50s and '60s in the state of Louisiana says a lot about the racial setting in the society of my youth. Jim Crow laws were fully in force during those years, and the racial divide was wide, understood by those on both sides of that chasm and accepted as a part of our way of life. The Civil Rights Movement kicked into full swing during my teen years, but prior to that, racial segregation was firmly entrenched, along with its horrors.

Parents Who Weren't Racist

Thankfully, I managed to escape the worst of it by being blessed with parents who were somehow not racist. I'm sure that they must have observed many of the customs of the day in how that society functioned in its separateness, but I know that I didn't grow up with the commonly accepted attitudes toward African Americans that many of my friends and relatives possessed. I clearly had my mother and father to thank for that.

When I say that my parents weren't racist, I say it from the memories of my experiences with them and African Americans, not from being sat down and instructed about racism. I just remember that black people liked my mother and father, and I don't believe for a moment it was because they thought they had no choice in order to stay out of trouble. My father was a bricklayer, and back then all of the skilled labor force was composed of white men, and the common laborers who assisted them were black men. My father treated the laborers with respect, and it was obvious that they appreciated it.

Like many boys born in that era, I grew up loving the outdoors and did more than my fair share of hunting and fishing. My dad, an avid hunter and fisherman, knew which of the laborers at his job had knowledge of good places to hunt. At age nine, I shot my first squirrel. We were hunting on the property of a laborer named Jake, or perhaps he just had access to the property. At any rate, he was known for his hunting prowess, and my dad took me to hunt with him as our guide. Jake took me as his trainee of the day and helped me locate and shoot my squirrel. All I remember about the day is the one shot I made and the friendly relationship my dad had with Jake. My father was big on kids showing respect for adults, so for me, it was "Mr. Jake." I feel quite sure that my answering him was in my normal terms of "Yes Sir" and "No Sir." That was not the norm for most white kids, by the way, in addressing black folks. Jake was tickled to be the one to help me enjoy my first hunting success, almost as excited as I was.

A Special "Man"

When I was perhaps twelve or thirteen, I had a great-uncle do me a great favor, in spite of the fact that his racial prejudice was obvious. My great-uncle didn't hunt, but he loved me and knew how much I loved to hunt. Thus, he introduced me to an older black man with the last name of Hollingsworth who owned a hunting dog. They all lived in the "sticks" as we called it, deep in the piney woods of Louisiana about a hundred miles from my home. I loved it there and went to visit every time I had the chance (and I *made* many chances).

Mr. Hollingsworth just went by the name "Man." I think his name might have been John, but I never knew for sure. He just told me to call him Man, and he called me Gordon—friends on a first-name basis. In the 1950s, do I have to mention that this was a very unusual relationship for a white kid? Older black people were often expected to say "Mr. Bob" (or whatever their first names were) to teenagers. That sounds weird to the younger generation now, but sadly, it was common when I was a teen (although not appealing to me personally at all). That is why I say that my relationship with Man was both special and unusual.

By the time I started hunting with Man, he was somewhere on the other side of seventy years old. He was a widower and lived in a very small, plain house. I suspect he was quite poor financially, likely surviving on small Social Security checks. I remember that there was no grass in his yard and no paint on his little house. But the inside of his house was immaculately kept. He didn't have much, but what he had was well cared for. I honestly don't think he liked much of anything about hunting at his stage of life, but he "took a liking" to me and took me hunting any time I wanted to go.

He would invite me over for breakfast and cook a very nice, delicious breakfast. Thinking back to that brings me both joy and pain. I loved it, but it must have put a burden on his very low income. We built a special bond by spending many days hunting from daylight to dark together. When I think of that part of the state, where quite a few of my relatives once lived, the memory of Man ushers in the most emotional pain. I really miss him. I wish I could have known what I know now, for perhaps I would have found more ways to encourage him.

A Hard First Job

As I mentioned in a previous chapter, when I graduated from the ninth grade, my father informed me that he had a summer job lined up for me. That was a day of bad news. I wanted to fish and swim all summer with my buddies, like I usually did. But remember that my dad was old-school, which is actually a serious understatement. "Yes Sir," I replied. I started an eight-year-long summer job track, working as a laborer for bricklayers and carpenters. That put me in the role of working with black men. It was a strenuous job during those hot, muggy Louisiana summers. We had to build scaffolds for the bricklayers, stack them with bricks, mix mortar and keep the mortar boards filled with it, plus do various other related jobs. The maximum number of workers was supposed to be two laborers for every three bricklayers, but on my first job, we had four bricklayers for two of us to keep up with. It was a long, hot summer for a fifteen-year-old.

Those summer jobs continued through high school and college, and sometimes during school breaks, all alongside the black guys. Both they and I thought it was pretty cool. They respected my work ethic and liked my crazy humor, and I loved hanging out with them. I had a recent realization about those days that was rather surprising: in those eight years, I was the only white kid that ever worked as a common laborer on those jobs, and some of the jobs were big ones with many such workers. I know the other skilled labor guys had kids my age, and I know that they didn't have any more money than my family had, but I was the only white boy who did it. Those other fathers saw me working every summer and could have gotten their sons similarly employed—but they didn't. Why was that? The only answer that makes sense is that their racial prejudice blocked them from being willing to have their sons work with black guys. That recent realization makes me appreciate my father even more.

A Different Mother Too

Looking back, it makes sense that I have been comfortable with black people for as long as I can remember. Daddy didn't have social relationships with African Americans off the job, except for hunting, but they respected him and he respected them. My mother was no different. We didn't have much money, but at times we would have a black lady come to our house to help with the ironing. Mother's relationships with them were nothing like the mess in the movie, *The Help.* They laughed and joked together, and I suspect had their teatimes together. Mom just loved people—of all types.

I remember one day our ironing lady couldn't find anyone to leave her son with, so she brought him to our house with her. He and I were about the same age, probably ten or eleven years old. It must have been in the summertime, since we weren't in school, but we had a fun day together. We went out in the front yard and played tackle football most of the day. That's not easy with such small teams, but we did it—tackling and wrestling each other for hours on end. What did the neighbors think of this unusual sight? I don't know and didn't even think about it then, and certainly my mother didn't care. So you see, when I say that my parents weren't racist, I think the facts speak for themselves. Thank you, Mother!

Perhaps you wonder if I wrote this chapter to give myself a pat on the back because I had relationships with some black people in a day when that was quite unusual. No, that wasn't my reason for writing it, not at all. I was a very worldly, sinful young man who didn't deserve pats on the back. I wrote this only to demonstrate what those times were like in my childhood and youth and to describe why I am so thankful to have been raised as I was— without racist attitudes. The pats on the back are reserved for my mother, my father, the black folks who were willing to befriend me, and God. Somehow by his grace, I escaped one sin at least, racism, and I am most grateful.

Into Heart and Life

1. Think back to what your early memories are about those of different races, and how the significant people in your life viewed them. Any surprises?

2. Do you have close friends of other races who would agree with you and also say that they are close friends of yours? (NOTE: There is a big difference between friendly acquaintances and close friends.)

3. Commit to reading two books by Michael Burns: *Crossing the Line: Culture, Race, and Kingdom* and *All Things to All People.* I promise that you will be very thankful that you did it!

8

My Diverse Spiritual Family

In the last days
the mountain of the LORD's temple will be established
as chief among the mountains;
it will be raised above the hills,
and peoples will stream to it.
Many nations will come and say,

"Come, let us go up to the mountain of the LORD,
to the temple of the God of Jacob.
He will teach us his ways,
so that we may walk in his paths."
—Micah 4:1-2a NIV1984

As I described in the previous chapter, I was comfortable around those of other races for as long as I can remember, and my parents were a big part of that. However, in the segregated setting in which I grew up in the Deep South, normal social relationships between races were pretty much nonexistent. Further, as has often been said, Sundays were the most segregated day of the week. There were white churches and black churches and never the twain did meet.

When my younger sister was in high school during the early 1970s, the schools were just starting to be integrated in our hometown of Shreveport, Louisiana. She and her friends from their church youth group were very evangelistic, and she reached out to her African American band director, who, along with his wife, ended up studying the Bible with some members of my sister's church. Amazingly, they were open to the study and to the Bible teachings being shared, and they both ended up being baptized and attending that white church. Sad to say, they didn't stay for long. I doubt that they encountered any direct racism, knowing that particular church, but I don't doubt that they felt extremely out of place. The white members simply didn't know how to bridge the racial gap socially. For me and my sister, that is an extremely sad memory.

The Most Segregated Day of the Week

By the time I had started my preaching career when in my upper twenties, little had changed regarding the racial composition of churches. I remember the first time I was invited to speak for a black church. I was both at ease and excited. I supposed that my comfortability with black folks was due to the experiences of my early years, but in retrospect, I now think my gene pool was involved to at least some extent. More on that in a moment.

Although our churches of the same doctrinal beliefs remained almost entirely segregated, in one location we did have monthly preachers' luncheons with ministers from both groups present. The fellowship was great in those settings. We leaders did attend special meetings at times in each other's congregations, which was always positive, but somehow, we were missing the bigger picture. The promise made to Abraham back in Genesis 12 was that all peoples would be blessed through his lineage. The Great Commission of Matthew 28:19 directed the spread of the gospel to all nations. Most nations now include a mixture of those from many other countries, and certainly that is true of the country in which I live. The mystery of Christ described by Paul in Ephesians 3:2–5 was that racial divisions would end in Christ's kingdom. In fact, the blending of the nations into one spiritual body is the demonstration of the power of Christ's cross.

Prior to joining what I then called the Discipling Movement in the mid-80s, my last mainline type church was centered in a military neighborhood. Thus, we were more diverse than most churches in that fellowship of churches—and more diverse than most of those same churches are even today. That was a special blessing. Once I had become a part of the fellowship of churches I am now in, racial diversity was a given. Of course, racial diversity in membership doesn't mean that racial diversity outside of assemblies exists in the ways it should. I cover topics like that one in my blogsite, blacktaxandwhitebenefits.com.

The Big Black Brothers' Club

The BBB Club

While I was writing this very chapter, a black friend from Boston called me unexpectedly. Walter Parrish is his name, and he, along with six others, became a part of the group called the *Big Black Brothers' Club* (the BBBs). I have a chapter by that title in my book *The Power of Spiritual Thinking,* also found as an article on both my Bible teaching website (gordonferguson.org) and my racial topics blogsite (blacktaxandwhitebenefits.com). This unusual group had its origin in the 1990s in Boston, an origin that was based on a Monday night gathering of men to watch football games.

My house was the gathering place, and after months of church brothers coming over to watch the game, I casually made an observation in these words: "Hey, we're all black here." In today's verbiage, I would have said, "We're all black up in here." At any rate, someone suggested that our group of regulars call ourselves the Big Black Brothers' Club, and we did. Since I was the only paleface present, the other six voted me black on Monday nights and presented me with an official-looking certificate to that effect. It was quite the group—a loud, raucous, rowdy group who knew how to let our hair down (to put it mildly)! After all these years, I stay in touch with the original brothers, although two have already graduated to glory. Walter was calling to plan a gathering at my house in Dallas to spend the upcoming Super Bowl weekend together. Although the plans were made, we had to postpone our gathering due to Walter undergoing an emergency surgery. But when we do meet, it will be quite a reunion, since I have now been gone from Boston for the same length of years I lived there (sixteen).

My DNA Test!

Toward the end of decade one of this century, I was providentially blessed to get tied in with a sister church in Houston for a couple of years. I think the membership was about half black and the leadership similar. On my first trip there to conduct a special workshop for the singles ministry, I made the same statement I have been making for decades, namely, "I must have some black blood because I have too much soul to be a white man!" One of the elders, a black brother, said to me during that weekend that I could take a DNA test to find out if I was right or not about my gene pool. His challenge scared me, honestly. What if I didn't have any black heritage in my gene pool? That would have been a big disappointment.

Toward the end of my time working with this church, I finally took the DNA test—with fear and trepidation. You can read about the results in an article on both my website and blogsite. If you are an old movie buff, the title of the article gives it away: "Surprise, Surprise: Guess Who's Been Coming to Dinner!" The article is as humorous in tone as the title, but it contains some seriously painful material also. The other articles on my blogsite, which are written mostly by me but include some by other authors, are of a more serious nature, given our history and current racial climate in America.

Color-Aware and Color-Appreciative

My current home church in Dallas, Texas, is a diverse one, although not as diverse as the one in Houston. Since our members are scattered all over the Dallas-Fort Worth Metroplex, we are organized into three regional groups. One of the groups is almost exactly half white and half nonwhite, and the ministry staff has a similar composition. I could not imagine being a part of a predominantly white church now. Jesus said that the world would recognize true disciples by their love for one another and by their unity (John 13 and John 17). Having a racially diverse church in a southern city reflecting these two qualities is the greatest advertisement imaginable for true Christianity. Not having this composition makes the opposite statement.

I have considered writing a whole book about my black friends and shared experiences through the years. I can hardly write chapters like these last two, because my mind keeps being flooded with all the precious memories built with those friends in these experiences. Sometimes my white friends make the mistake of saying that they are colorblind. That would mean that color doesn't count—but it does! I am very color-aware and color-appreciative. My life has been enriched by having friends who were very different from me in many ways, color included. From my early years, God has blessed me through these differences. In the last thirty-plus years, he has blessed me by leading me to a fellowship of churches characterized by racial and cultural diversity. For all those blessings and the added blessings growing out of them, I am most grateful!

Into Heart and Life

1. We cannot help carry the burdens of others if we do not know what they are (Galatians 6:2). If you are white, ask at least five people of color what life is like in their world on the racial front.

2. Understanding the need to share your own burdens with others, if you are a person of color, initiate conversations with at least five white persons to find out how they view racial differences and racial tensions in our present society. Make sure to tell them "your" story.

3. Set up social times with those of a different color/culture than you in the next two months. Expand your comfort zones and friendship zones.

9

Building on Broken Dreams and Closed Doors

> *Then Joseph said to his brothers, "come close to me."*
> *When they had done so, he said, "I am your brother*
> *Joseph, the one you sold into Egypt! And now, do not*
> *be distressed and do not be angry with yourselves for*
> *selling me here, because it was to save lives that god*
> *sent me ahead of you. For two years now there has*
> *been famine in the land, and for the next five years*
> *there will be no plowing and reaping. But god sent me*
> *ahead of you to preserve for you a remnant on earth*
> *and to save your lives by a great deliverance.*
> *"so then, it was not you who sent me here, but god.*
> —Genesis 45:4-8

I once heard a leader say that the kingdom of God is built on dreams. After a pregnant pause, he finished the thought—*broken* dreams. We are easily excited by the thought of having kingdom dreams and seeing our lives affect eternity by our doing great things (by God's power, of course!). What happens when God doesn't give us those dreams, or worse, seems about to give them to us and then takes them back with a flourish?

About now it would be good to think of the old country and western song title, "Thank God for Unanswered Prayers." Sometimes God closes doors that he knows will be bad for us. Sometimes he closes doors because he has a better door to open. Either way, we are going to have to learn not only to endure disappointments in seeing our dreams and plans denied, but also to be thankful when it happens, believing that God is in control and going to do better things for us through those disappointments.

In a later chapter, I've written about my initial disappointment and the pain it brought into my heart when my first plan to go back to school to train for the ministry didn't work out. When God decided to open that door, he did it suddenly and shockingly. That story is described in detail in Chapter 7 of my little book My Three Lives. The growth spiritually in having to wrestle with God during that trial was worth the pain. But the door God opened was such a better door in myriad ways. Beautiful! Thank you, Lord! Easy to say after the better door is opened, but difficult to say at the time the first one is slammed and locked shut.

Paul and Closed Doors

Paul was quite well acquainted with this process. I think he learned quickly to be thankful for closed doors, by faith awaiting the opening of a new, improved one. Acts 16 gives us two examples of closed and open doors that are pretty amazing to contemplate. Here is the first one:

Paul and his companions traveled throughout the region of Phrygia and Galatia, having been kept by the Holy Spirit from preaching the word in the province of Asia. When they came to the border of Mysia, they tried to enter Bithynia, but the spirit of Jesus would not allow them to. So they passed by Mysia and went down to Troas. During the night Paul had a vision of a man of Macedonia standing and begging him, "Come over to Macedonia and help us." After Paul had seen the vision, we got ready at once to leave for Macedonia, concluding that God had called us to preach the gospel to them. (Acts 16:6-10)

It certainly made sense to try and go to Asia. That is where Ephesus was located and the very location Paul went to on his third journey. From there, all Asia was evangelized (Acts 19:10). The churches written to in Revelation 2 and 3 were among those churches started from Paul's mission base in Ephesus. But that was all a part of his third mission trip. The Holy Spirit closed the door on Asia when Paul was on his second missionary journey. Another door was closed shortly thereafter when they tried to enter Bithynia. Then the right door opened, and the indication of Paul's faith in both closed and open doors is found in the phrase, "We got ready at once to leave for Macedonia."

Later in Acts 16, another door was closed shockingly hard. It is described in these verses:

After they had been severely flogged, they were thrown into prison, and the jailer was commanded to guard them carefully. Upon receiving such orders, he put them in the inner cell and fastened their feet in the stocks.

About midnight Paul and Silas were praying and singing hymns to God, and the other prisoners were listening to them. Suddenly there was such a violent earthquake that the foundations of the prison were shaken. At once all the prison doors flew open, and everyone's chains came loose. The jailer woke up, and when he saw the prison doors open, he drew his sword and was about to kill himself because he thought the prisoners had escaped. But Paul shouted, "Don't harm yourself! We are all here!"

The jailer called for lights, rushed in and fell trembling before Paul and Silas. He then brought them out and asked, "Sirs, what must I do to be saved?" (Acts 16:23-30)

Paul's faith in closed doors was at its height in Philippi. After being stripped and beaten, he and Silas were praying and singing hymns to God. Can you imagine what most of us might be thinking and saying under such circumstances? "Here we are just trying to serve God and preach the good news, yet this is what happens! Where is the justice in all of this, anyway?" Having faith in closed doors is a process of spiritual vision that begins with a decision based on the nature of God. He is good and he has a plan for our lives, and further, he is going to carry it out in ways that we likely cannot guess. He is insistent that we learn to walk by faith and not by sight, and closed doors are a part of that learning process.

A Painful Loss of a Dream

Another story of a closed door and broken dream in my life is found in Chapter 9 of My Three Lives. That door was open enough for us to put a down payment on a house in Seattle. It is quite the story, one that shook me spiritually but ended up well. Since the Three Lives book documents my own spiritual journey, several stories with similar themes are found in it. One that was difficult to digest at the time was having the door closed to lead the church planting to Dallas back in 1990. I had become an elder in Boston and was told that serving in that role in that church was a higher priority than planting Dallas as an evangelist. Honestly, that put me into a grief process that lasted the better part of a year.

As I was describing that situation to a friend after moving to Dallas in 2015, he asked what I thought about that closed door in retrospect. Oddly, I'm not sure I had ever thought about it in those terms. Upon doing so, it was obviously a wonderful closed door. Had we not stayed in Boston for the sixteen years we were there, I likely wouldn't have written the books I have written. I for sure would not have enjoyed more than a decade of working with the young churches in Europe that we made frequent trips to, to help and strengthen them. I wouldn't have taught all the ministry training classes in New England and Europe that I was blessed to teach. I wouldn't have lived in Paris for six months in 1999 to help the church there build a better atmosphere of family. That list could go on and on.

Better Dreams and Better Doors

God doesn't make mistakes, and if we are willing servants, all closed doors will lead to better ones being opened. He builds us and his family on our broken dreams and closed doors as a part of a divine plan to mold us into faith walkers. We may long for the easy ways and the obvious ways, but spiritual growth doesn't come in those forms. It comes by facing challenges with faith in a God who moves in mysterious ways his wonders to perform. When the dreams get dashed and the doors slammed shut, get ready for something exciting to happen! God is just about to do his thing in your life once again. Look up to heaven and enjoy the ride—it's a'coming!

Into Heart and Life

1. List your three most painful broken dreams and closed doors, what you learned from each and what you still might need to do with them.

2. With the old country and western song title in mind, what are some of your unanswered prayers for which you are most thankful in retrospect?

3. Do your disappointments in life tend to become stumbling blocks to your faith or steppingstones to greater faith? If the former, how can you change your reactions?

10

Life's Endgame and the
Greatest Story Ever Told

He was in the world, and though the world was made through him, the world did not recognize him. He came to that which was his own, but his own did not receive him. Yet to all who did receive him, to those who believed in his name, he gave the right to become children of God—children born not of natural descent, nor of human decision or a husband's will, but born of God.

The Word became flesh and made his dwelling among us. We have seen his glory, the glory of the one and only Son, who came from the Father, full of grace and truth.

—John 1:10-14

Aging and death are realities of life on planet earth, and those realities are viewed by virtually all of us as negative, usually very negative. From the perspective of 1 Corinthians 15:26, death is the last enemy to be destroyed at the general resurrection of the dead. The term "enemy" pretty well sums up how we view death, right? Aging is a necessary part of the process that culminates in death. We humans don't enjoy aging, with its attendant strains and pains, and we don't enjoy thinking about our demise. Those are facts. Yet is there another perspective that can change how we view those facts, making them seem less negative for sure and possibly even positive? That's a very good question to ponder, don't you think?

In 2016, Jeanie Shaw served as an author and editor of an amazing book entitled *An Aging Grace.* Using a group of older authors, important topics related to aging are covered in very biblical and practical ways. Younger people should read the book to help them deal with their older friends and relatives, and older people should read it to help prepare themselves for the inevitabilities coming their way. In my opinion, this book should be a must-read for all followers of Christ.

I wrote two chapters for the book and in the first of these, here were two sentences describing my initial reaction to the request to write them: "Jeanie Shaw, whose brainchild this book is, asked me to write two chapters: one about getting old and the other about dying. (She says the topic was 'heaven,' but I heard 'dying.')... My initial reaction was 'What? Why me? How did I get those two topics anyway? I hate getting old and I'm afraid to die!'" I think the chapters ended up being good ones, and it helped me to write them. But I have continued to think about aging and death as a person now in my upper seventies. This present chapter describes my most profound thoughts on the subject at this point in my life.

Our Attachment to the Physical

We are attached to this physical world and we are attached because God made us to be. We were created to enjoy life on this earth. It offers amazing possibilities—some amazingly bad and some amazingly good. David described the good part in this way:

> *Come, my children, listen to me;*
> *I will teach you the fear of the LORD.*
> *Whoever of you loves life*
> *and desires to see many good days,*

keep your tongue from evil
    and your lips from telling lies.
Turn from evil and do good;
    seek peace and pursue it. (Psalm 34:11-14)

Peter quoted this passage in 1 Peter 3:10-12. Loving life in this physical body and desiring to see good days, many of them, is not wrong. In fact, it would be wrong to feel otherwise. James said that "every good and perfect gift is from above" (James 1:17), and that includes life in this physical world. That is why we should give thanks for every one of those good gifts that we enjoy while in this body. One of those obvious delights is food, created for our enjoyment and thanksgiving (1 Timothy 4:3-5), just like all other physical things that we call good.

Further, God made us to want to remain alive as long as possible. The Bible is full of examples showing that his righteous people fought hard to remain alive. Finding anyone who wanted to die at the moment is nearly impossible to do. Those who can be found were looking for an escape from intense suffering, although Paul seemed to be an exception, based on what he wrote in Philippians 1:21-23. But a closer examination of that context shows that although he knew death was better because he could be with Christ, he went on to say that he wanted to remain alive in order to fulfill his purpose of helping others. Add to that the fact that he had seen both a resurrected Jesus and the spiritual world beyond (2 Corinthians 12:1-7). He thus was given a perspective that we have to work hard to develop and then keep—by faith, not by sight.

Life with Spiritual Purpose

Paul knew that his purpose was to use his life to help others know and love God. Life on earth is a preparation for heaven, and finding purpose is a large part of that preparation. Discovering the answers to the biggest questions in life is a part of the process. Three of the biggest questions are these: where did I come from; where am I going; and what am I doing here? Humans instinctively search for the answers to these questions because of our very nature. We are made in the image of God, and this makes our search for meaning inevitable, because it is actually our search for him.

He wants us to search for our origin, which is him. He wants us to search for our destiny, which is with him. He wants us to search for our purpose, because it is our way of having fellowship with him in his mission for saving the people on this earth. Having the purpose of representing him to those people means that we want to live and not die until he knows that our purpose has been fulfilled. Acts 13:36 nails it: "Now when David had served God's purpose in his own generation, he fell asleep..." Thus, wanting to stay alive and enjoy life is our designed nature. It is not necessarily a sign of being unspiritual or too attached to this world (although it can be).

Yet a part of the right mixture is the anticipation of heaven and an "otherworldly" absence of the fear of death. Before Christ's death and resurrection, even spiritual people in the Old Testament era were "held in slavery by their fear of death" for their entire lives (Hebrews 2:14–15). We should now view life and death differently than those who lived before the cross. Picture it this way— imagine a person who loves their job and has a strong assurance of job security. Although they look forward to and anticipate their retirement greatly, they put their heart into their job every day and do it excellently. The faith-filled disciple of Jesus is very similar in how they view life, their purpose in it and their future. They are comfortable both with the present and comfortable anticipating the future, including death. They are in all ways quite like the child described in Psalm 131:2: "But I have calmed and quieted myself, I am like a weaned child with its mother; like a weaned child I am content." Such a person ideally accepts both aging and death with peace and not with fear or mere perseverance with gritted teeth. But just how do we reach that ideal?

The Worst Story Ever Told

We reach it by really grasping the big picture, the biggest possible, as fully as is humanly possible—the greatest story ever told. Just what do you think this is? Common answers are good but often incomplete, such as God's love or Jesus on the cross bearing our sins, and other variations or additions to these two. The biggest picture goes much deeper and must start at the dawn of creation.

Adam and Eve were created perfect in just about every way, and they were certainly sinless. Once sin entered the world, a slowly developing whirlpool for humanity had begun and there was no stopping it. The rate of its swirling might have seemed to have paused at times in history, but not for long. Ultimately, it would pick up speed and pull every human being into its deadly vortex. The consequences of sin are many, but death is at the center— both spiritual death (separation from God) and physical death (separation from our own bodies). Once banned from the Garden that housed the Tree of Life, the original pair began to age and head toward physical death, and that sentence of death had to include all humans from that point forward (Genesis 3:22–24). We each die spiritually because of our own sins, but we die physically because of that first sin in the Garden and the subsequent banishment from its Tree of Life.

The Greatest Story Ever Told

God by his nature is both all-knowing and timeless. He sees what we call time all at once—past, present and future. Before he created the world with humans as its apex, he knew exactly what was going to happen. He knew what the pain of rebellion was going to do to humankind and to him. His plan was clearly in place long before it was implemented. That plan was destined to become the greatest story ever told. The Creator was going to take the form of a creature in order to die and save his creatures for eternity. Who could ever have imagined such a story?

It is true that other religions have mythology that includes gods taking human forms, as shown in Acts 14:8–18, but no other religion would dare imagine that a god would die for his sinful, rebellious creatures. All religions have this in common: they teach that we should be good and do good. Christianity is totally unique in teaching that we cannot do this without divine intervention enabling us to; and that intervention began with God becoming human to die for all the sins of all humans of all time. Mind-boggling! Unbelievable! The greatest story ever imagined, and the greatest story ever told!

Christianity is absolutely unique. That uniqueness explains why these two statements are true of Christ's religion and true only of his religion:

Jesus answered, "I am the way and the truth and the life. No one comes to the Father except through me" (John 14:6).

"Salvation is found in no one else, for there is no other name under heaven given to mankind by which we must be saved" (Acts 4:12).

Once a group of theologians were discussing world religions and the question of whether Christianity was unique, and if so, why? C.S. Lewis, famous author and teacher of the last century, entered the group's discussion late. Upon hearing the topic, he stated quickly that the answer was simple: grace! The idea of grace is amazing, as the well-loved song puts it, but beyond amazing when you consider what made saving grace possible—God becoming man and dying for his creation that grace might abound! It was the only answer for the dilemma of sin and God knew it and did it.

Embracing the Near-Inconceivable

Now that I've begun to comprehend this big picture more fully, I would not want to eliminate my aging and death even if I somehow could. How could I possibly desire to rob the world of the greatest story ever told, which was the only way to save humanity spiritually? I believe I am now looking at that process differently than I did when I wrote those words in Aging Grace back in 2016, saying that I hated aging and was afraid to die. I keep applying myself to understanding my purpose in this last part of life. I must still be alive for a reason. God is not yet done with me.

A part of that reason is for me to keep trying to better understand and explain to others how to embrace life's endgame and all that it brings to us and to our friends and family whom we leave behind.

I have a deeper sense of peace about life's final chapter, a sense that I could often best describe as a peace that "transcends all understanding" (Philippians 4:7). In this chapter, I have tried to explain what simply must be considered the greatest story ever told. I pray that it helps your understanding of why aging and death are to be embraced, even joyfully. God knows that we need to help each other through that portal into an eternity that is quite literally inconceivable until we enter into it. The famous Christian song says, "I can only imagine," but actually, you cannot. The Great Beyond is quite greatly beyond our wildest imagination. Near the end of *Aging Grace*, I wrote these words, providing an apt way to close this chapter:

> Life in the womb of this earth is sometimes comfortable and peaceful, and the thought of leaving it might still be a bit scary. But let's allow it to be scary in the same way that astronauts must feel as the flames of rocket fuel start pushing them into a world they have heretofore only imagined.

With that, I close this chapter. I'll see you there, maybe soon!

Into Heart and Life

1. How do you view aging and death—honestly? Think carefully.

2. How do those topics relate to your present spirituality level and view of God?

3. In what ways is your thinking and feeling about life's endgame affected by reflecting on the greatest story ever told?

11

God's Unlimited Patience and Forgiveness

But for that very reason I was shown mercy so that in me, the worst of sinners, Christ Jesus might display his unlimited patience as an example for those who would believe on him and receive eternal life. (1 Timothy 1:16 NIV1984)

—1 Timothy 1:16 NIV1984

The word "unlimited" in the translation quoted above is a very common one meaning "all," "every" or "total." It is translated in various ways, as "immense" in the newer version of the NIV and "perfect" in the NASB. However it is translated, the concept is amazing, almost unbelievable. How can God be this patient with us as sinners, for we all fall short of his perfect will every day? Understanding the extent of his grace is impossible until we have a good grasp of the extent of our sins, but here is a fair warning: seeing how sinful we truly are makes it harder to fully trust that his grace and forgiveness really will cover all our sins.

Let's start by understanding the broad scope of our sins. Without listing the many specific types of sins that we could, consider the general headings or categories into which they fall. Obviously, we sin by the wrong things that we do, our actions. 2 Corinthians 5:10 says that these sins will be brought before the judgment seat of

Christ. We also sin through our words (Matthew 12:36), which are said here to also be a part of what we must give account for on the Judgment Day. Next comes our thought life through which we also sin (Mark 7:21); these sins arise from our hearts. Then comes our inner motives (1 Corinthians 4:5), which will be brought to light at the coming of Christ. In this verse, Paul also mentions that our hidden sins will be revealed; and most of our sins are hidden from others.

Only we know the scope of our sins of thought and motive, and those are our most common types of sins. How would you feel about having your thought life during the last six months projected in detail on a screen before an audience of your friends and relatives and a thousand more? Add to these overwhelming categories of sins our sins of omission (James 4:17), the things that we should have done and didn't do, and we can wonder how anyone can be saved, especially us. Right?

The Accuser and Deceiver

It is important to understand how Satan uses our own consciences against us. Revelation 12:9–10 informs us that he both deceives us and accuses us. From a personal conscience perspective, some of us are deceived about our own sins and don't understand how big a sinner we really are. That fact explains why God warns us about thinking that we don't have sin in 1 John 1:8–9, a warning that follows one of the most reassuring verses in the New Testament about God's forgiveness. In verse 7, we are promised that walking in the light with God means that our sins are being continuously washed away in the blood of Christ.

However, most of us who are trying to please God are not deceived by Satan into being blind to our sins. Rather, our consciences are so accused that we have a difficult time fully accepting forgiveness, especially right after examining the passages about sin already mentioned—and these are but a few of the staggering number of sin passages that could be listed. Just about now, the question bursts forth from our hearts, almost screaming for an answer:

"How could we possibly be forgiven of the millions of sins we must have committed in a lifetime?"

That is where the promises come in about God having unlimited patience and complete forgiveness. But how can we get our minds and hearts around his promise to forgive all our sins (Colossians 2:13) and thus to save us *completely* (Hebrews 7:25)? As one with a highly accused conscience, I have wrestled with such questions for much of my life. That perhaps explains why the Book of Romans has been so important to me and why I have taught it so many times in so many places (plus written a book about it). Like many before me, it has been my go-to Bible book for help in accepting God's mercy and minimizing my fear of him and of the Judgment Day. Here are three very practical concepts that have brought peace to my heart in this matter.

Humans and Forgiveness

One, I look at humans and their capacity to forgive others. It is nothing short of astounding. When you put it into the realm of parents forgiving children and children forgiving parents, it is especially remarkable. The father in the Prodigal Son story of Luke 15 (representing God) is not unique, by any means. Earthly parents long for the return of estranged children and are looking to the horizon constantly for any indication that they might come back. The forgiveness I have received from my wife of fifty-five years is off the charts. You can see this "unlimited" and "immense" capacity to show mercy in yourself and countless others.

If humans have this capacity and are anxious to use it in dealing with family and loved ones, just where do you think the capacity came from in the first place? Whatever good qualities we have came from God and are but faint reflections of those same qualities in him. The amounts and types of forgiveness I see in God's creatures helps me tremendously in grasping what I know must reside in his very nature. He delights to show mercy and forgiveness, and his immense patience allows him to do it in ways beyond our comprehension. Relax a bit now, and just decide to accept that fact. God is good, and he loves you enough to die for you—and he already did. Accept him and his forgiveness.

Commands Show God's Infinite Capacity

Two, I look at what he has commanded us to do with each other. In Colossians 3:13, we are told to forgive each other as he has forgiven us. Numerous other passages say the same thing. Forgiveness of others is commanded in no uncertain terms, over and over again. As Peter was beginning to get the concept Jesus was teaching, he asked if he should forgive up to seven times (Matthew 18:21). In the next verse, Jesus said that we should forgive seventy-seven times (in other words, unlimited forgiveness). In Luke 17:4, Jesus used the number seven, but said that we should be prepared to forgive someone that many times in one day! The apostles were staggered by that command, and instantly cried out, "Increase our faith!" (verse 5). The point is this: God would not require us humans to forgive so extensively if he didn't already do the same thing—and far more. Rest assured that God asks nothing good of us that he is not absolutely perfect at doing himself. Thus, he is perfect at forgiveness. That thought calms my accused heart and I pray that it does yours.

Jesus, Master of Forgiveness

Three, look at Jesus' example as he lived among us. Sometimes studying the Old Testament gives me the wrong kind of fear of God. You see much grace in the Old Testament, but you also see what can easily appear as harshness in God's dealings with humankind. The Old Testament is not designed to give us a complete picture of God and his nature, although it has many important purposes. Jesus came to earth as a human to explain God and his nature. "No one has ever seen God, but the one and only Son, who is himself God and is in closest relationship with the Father, has made him known" (John 1:18). The Greek term translated "made him known" in this version is the word from which we get our word "exegesis." Hence, Jesus has exegeted God—fully explained him in his very personhood. In John 14:8, Philip asked Jesus to show them the

Father, to which Jesus answered in amazement, "Don't you know me, Philip, even after I have been among you such a long time? Anyone who has seen me has seen the Father. How can you say, 'Show us the Father'?"

What did the apostles (and many others) see in Jesus? To mention but a few instances, in John 4 Jesus struck up a conversation with a Samaritan woman (violating cultural norms in at least two ways). As Jesus was talking with her about spiritual matters, he suggested that she bring her husband back with her to avail themselves of living water. At this point, she said that she had no husband, to which Jesus replied that she had been married to five different men and was currently shacked up with another guy to whom she was not married. Wow—quite the revelation, that! He did not shame her or rebuke her but rather continued the spiritual conversation, with the ultimate effect on her that she successfully evangelized a large number of people in her town.

Caught in the Act!

A similar account involved an incident in which a woman with loose morals was a part of a staged situation designed to test Jesus. Of course, I refer to the woman caught in the very act of adultery (John 8). The previous woman must have been quite embarrassed by Jesus' comment about her marital status (lack thereof). Sexual immorality was strongly taught against in both the Old and New Testaments. To be exposed even in words was humiliating, but to be exposed by being dragged out of the bed during intercourse and thrown before a crowd in the very presence of Jesus was the almost unimaginable height of humiliation. Imagine yourself in those circumstances and it will take your breath away! How did Jesus handle this situation that was beyond awkward? In a way that we don't fully understand, he dispelled the crowd, then he dismissed the shamed woman with gentle words: "Jesus straightened up and asked her, 'Woman, where are they? Has no one condemned you?' 'No one, sir,' she said. 'Then neither do I condemn you,' Jesus declared. 'Go now and leave your life of sin.'" Countless people have been drawn initially to Jesus by reading these words. That brand of grace is indeed immense and unlimited.

Finally, let's look at Peter again. Forgiving those closest to you can be the most difficult, as Proverbs 18:19 says in these words: "A brother wronged is more unyielding than a fortified city." Peter, after having received much grace already from Jesus, denied him three times, finally with an oath. Just after he had done it, he turned to see Jesus looking at him heartbroken (Matthew 26:69–75; Luke 22:54–62). After the resurrection, how did Jesus relate to Peter? What consequences did Jesus inflict upon him for this grievous sin? Although he had a little fireside chat with Peter in the last part of John 21, Peter was still the one selected to be the primary spokesman on the Day of Pentecost when the church was established (Acts 2) and was appointed to be the special apostle to the Jews, no doubt to Peter's amazement. Grace is amazing, isn't it? That's why the most popular Christian song is Amazing Grace!

Hopefully, these three practical insights have helped you deal with an accused conscience, if you are one of us with such a conscience. Sometimes just reading the multitude of biblical promises of forgiveness can become almost too familiar, although we should read them over and over and memorize a fair number of them. But when you need a little extra encouragement, think of our human capacity to forgive and where that capacity came from. Think of God's commands for us to forgive and realize that he never asks anything of us that he doesn't do perfectly himself and then enable us to do. Finally, just look at Jesus, the exegesis of God in the flesh. Amazing grace, how sweet the sound, that saved a wretch like me!

Into Heart and Life

1. Are you someone with an accused conscience or a deceived one? Why did you answer as you did?

2. What about your family and religious backgrounds might play a part in how your conscience functions?

3. What in this chapter was most helpful to you, and what will you do practically to find God's peace in your heart?

12

Safe Places, Safe People

The purposes of a person's heart are deep waters,
but one who has insight draws them out.

—Proverbs 20:5

Many years ago, our good friends, John and Karen Louis, requested a lunch time with us while we all were attending a church conference together. Their children were quite young at the time and they had a question about parenting. It went like this: "If you had to choose one principle of parenting as the most important, what would it be?" You might think trying to distill down all the important principles into one would be impossible, but the answer seemed immediately obvious. My answer: "Disciple the heart and not the behavior."

Of course, that answer was given in the form of a hyperbole, since parents do have to address behavior, especially when the children are very young. The point is that you can focus on behavior and gain outward compliance without changing the heart. Many parents make that mistake. I made it when my children were young. My answer in this case came from what I learned in the church later in life about discipling God's children. The principles are much the same, which means working with the heart is the most important part of being a parent or a people-helper in general. One can do the works of a servant without having the heart of a servant, but if one has the heart of a servant, they will do the works of a servant.

When we returned from that conference trip, I started asking my ministry friends what they thought was involved in discipling the heart. Some of the answers were alarming to me, focused on what seemed to be Bible lectures rather than really getting into the heart. The verse from Proverbs quoted above should provide us some common-sense guidance. What is hidden in our hearts must be drawn out by someone who gains our trust. Thus, my revised, longer answer to the Louis' question would go like this now: Disciple the heart and not simply the behavior, but realize that you must know what is in the heart before it can be discipled, and that finding out what is in the heart demands that you must be a safe place for the one you are trying to help.

Defining Discipling

This thing we call discipling is much more about asking questions and guiding others to their own conclusions than it is about giving answers. We are not trying to do the thinking for another person but aiming at helping them learn to think biblically and to do what Jesus would have them do. Being a safe person in a safe environment leads others to open their hearts to you. Parents who can do that with their children at a young age have a reasonable chance of keeping the lines of communication open when their children reach those more challenging teen years.

Several things are involved in developing such safe environments, including the assurance of confidentiality. Emotional calmness that doesn't react to news that might be shocking is also essential. If you ever say to someone trying to be vulnerable with you anything like "You did what?" you may never regain their trust. Even when the person is being honest about something they have against you, you cannot afford to take it personally and react. In such a situation, they are likely finding it difficult to be honest with you, and their manner may not be the best. In fact, it might be really bad and hurtful. Thankfully, Paul gives us some wonderful advice about how to handle even the worst of personal attacks. Read this passage carefully.

> *Don't have anything to do with foolish and stupid arguments, because you know they produce quarrels. And the Lord's servant must not be quarrelsome but must be kind to everyone, able to teach, not resentful. Opponents must be gently instructed, in the hope that God will grant them repentance leading them to a knowledge of the truth, and that they will come to their senses and escape from the trap of the devil, who has taken them captive to do his will. (2 Timothy 2:23-26)*

What are Paul's main points here? First, don't get pulled into arguments and quarrels. Stay calm and listen without reacting emotionally. Second, remain kind no matter what you may be hearing as you keep on trying to reason logically and biblically with the one attacking you, and don't take what they are saying personally and thus become resentful. Third, remain gentle in your attempts to reason with the other person by recognizing that they are out of their senses emotionally. Fourth, keep praying that God works in their heart, for ultimately, changing hearts is the Holy Spirit's job, not yours.

Expecting the Worst

Thankfully, I have been blessed with friends who understood how the principles in this passage worked as they have talked me off the emotional ledges I have been on at times. For me, no one did it better than my friend Wyndham, about whom I have written in previous chapters. I remember another highlight time with another old friend, Tom Brown. At the time, Tom was serving as the lead evangelist of the Boston church, and I was leading one of the ministry groups in that church. I was frustrated and upset about a number of things in my ministry and regarding the church in general. I decided to go over to Tom's house and tell him everything that was festering in my heart. If I had been a garbage truck, I could have not been more packed with refuse.

As I entered his house that night, I fully expected to be fired after dumping my load of bad attitudes on him. I was a mess and I acted like a mess. My manner and content were both terrible, and I didn't  hold back. I was angry and hurt and crying, and had no tissue to wipe my nose with. The whole occasion was messy to the max. At the end of my diatribe, I awaited a rebuke and my firing. Instead, Tom put his hand on my shoulder and said something very gentle and kind. That made the tears and the snot flow even more! It ended up a remarkable night, thanks to a remarkable man named Tom Brown—the very man responsible for getting me into this movement of churches in the first place.

Are you that kind of safe person for others? Can you calmly and lovingly draw out their hearts and help them get to better places emotionally and spiritually? I pray that you are able to do that, and if you are not now, I pray that you will devote yourself to becoming able. We all need help from others, and the safer you are perceived to be, the more you will be able to help people.

It's Your Decision

Another obvious point needs to be made here. We each are responsible to seek help in order to not only deal with our crises, but to keep growing as followers of the Christ. As important as finding safe persons to help in that continuing growth may be, we have to decide to trust others. I didn't trust Tom on the night just described—quite the contrary. But I knew that vulnerability, honesty and openness are not options for disciples. We must be open and honest despite the challenges it may bring.

The more we have endured pain at the hands of others, the greater the temptation to remain emotionally closed. But we cannot afford to let fear of hurt and rejection keep us from opening up. Most of our fears in relationships are imagined. Fellow Christians will be more accepting and loving than we think. Satan works hard to make us build false ideas about others in our minds. Don't let him. Believe that others will be a safe place to handle your heart. Be a safe place for others so that they will come to you in trust and vulnerability. Remember that the greatest compliment you can pay to another person is to open your heart to them. Just picture yourself pulling open the curtains of your heart and saying, "Here is the real me; please handle with care." Dedicate yourself to learning to do that with others and to helping them do it with you. It will lead to life-changing events, time after time. Regardless of whether you are on the giving or receiving end, you will end up overflowing with gratitude. Let's do it!

Into Heart and Life

1. What was your idea of discipling prior to reading this chapter and have you altered that idea after reading it? Explain your answer.

2. Are you able to remain calm when others verbally attack you (even though it may not be intended as that)? In other words, can you avoid taking things personally in an effort to help the other person get back in their right senses emotionally?

3. List those who are the safest people for you and those for whom you are a safe place. How can you expand your list in both directions?

13

Hurt by a Church Leader – Badly!

A brother wronged is more unyielding than a fortified city; disputes are like the barred gates of a citadel.

–Proverbs 18:19

Some of you reading this felt a sharp pain as you read the title of this chapter. I understand. We tend to put leaders on pedestals and thus we get deeply hurt when their humanness and sins affect us. The pain of disappointment is one of the sharpest pains of all. I hope to help you view your hurts in a different way. For starters, the ones we love most are those we hurt most and by whom we get hurt most. The deeper the love, the deeper the potential of pain. I have brought more pain into my wife's life than any other human, and she has done the same to me. Each of us has also brought more love into the other's life than anyone else.

The church leader God used to turn my life around 180 degrees did something before we really got to know each other that almost did me in spiritually, permanently. It involved one of my life's most embarrassing moments. My wife had been persistent in our first year of marriage in trying to get me involved in church. Although we had made an agreement to alternate between attending my type of church and her type, I soon reneged on our agreement. She then said that she would just go to my kind of church if I would only start going. Through the influence of some old friends our age, we started attending a church in our neighborhood.

A Slow Beginning

Although I wasn't much interested in church life, I saw in our friends some things that attracted me, particularly their marriage. We also shared a music background and interest that further pulled me in. I was a junior high school band director at the time, and he had been one in the recent past. He asked me to be the assistant director of a community band that he was starting. As our friendships in the church broadened, we started attending regularly, to Theresa's delight. I was even starting to feel like I might be able to develop into a church guy, a difficult thought to entertain in the early stages. Then, just as things were starting to come together, the preacher did something that was almost undoable in its potential consequences.

Theresa and I were both teachers, me a band teacher and she a sixth-grade teacher. Teacher pay has always been a topic of angst for teachers, and it was no different when we started teaching in the fall of 1965. Theresa's annual salary (for the nine-month school term) was $4400 and mine was $4620 (a bit extra for starting marching band early). I know that those are shocking figures, but adjusted for inflation, each of our salaries would come out to around $36,000 today. Our combined salaries, along with possible summer work, made life bearable financially. However, we had fully embraced the American Dream and were into amassing possessions. As a result, we were both doing a couple of part-time jobs in addition to our teaching jobs. All in all, we were making pretty good money and buying lots of stuff.

Almost an Abrupt Ending

One of my part-time jobs was playing music gigs of all sorts. I was in the musician's union and played in various seasonal music presentations, along with regular gigs in two dance bands and in the local symphony orchestra. One Sunday morning, Theresa and I were in the young marrieds Bible class taught by the preacher. He started talking about people's excuses for not attending midweek services, which we didn't at the time, mainly because symphony rehearsals were held on that night. But otherwise, I was growing in my interest and involvement with all things church related. As he continued his rant (that's how I perceived it), he said that one person would rather play in the symphony than attend church. Wow! I was the only person attending that church who played in the symphony. Everyone knew who he was talking about, although I learned later that he actually didn't know. He was just sharing what someone else told him, and if he heard the name at all, he probably didn't even know me at that point.

Whatever the case, it was one of my most embarrassing moments ever. I said nothing to anyone else about it, not even to Theresa, nor she to me. I suspect we were both embarrassed. After we left church, I took her home for her typical Sunday afternoon nap and told her I was going for a drive. As I drove around for hours, I was a mess. I cried and cried and most likely cursed and cursed. Just when church was starting to make sense to me, its main leader had humiliated me publicly. That was a very, very hard pill to swallow and an even harder one to digest. I wanted with all my heart to wash my hands of church forever, and I very nearly did. But by the time I finished my drive, I had decided to keep attending—for Theresa's sake. My reasoning was that although I was definitely going to hell now in my anger and bitterness, I didn't want to be responsible for taking her with me.

Great Pain Led to Great Gain

Funny how things turn out—unless you quit. By God's amazing providence in using my love for my wife, the story couldn't have had a better ending. I tell this story in some depth in Chapter 6 of *My Three Lives.* You should read it, or reread it. I picked up there with the part about starting to fish with Richard, the preacher and source of my early humiliation. It is an amazing story that brings

tears to my eyes every time I think about it (including now). I have always thought that, given my hard heart toward spiritual things, Richard was the only person in the whole state of Louisiana who could have gotten to me. I've said exactly that hundreds of times, and I believe it totally. God stuck him right in the middle of my life and wouldn't let me escape.

On one of our many fishing trips later, I shared that early incident with Rich. He wept like a baby. He had no idea what he had done. We cried together, shedding really good tears. I started to write here that as we did, the last of my pain dissipated. However, that wouldn't have been true. My pain had been gone for a long time. I knew that bitterness kills, and I had gained enough spirituality to give it up long before he even knew about it, much less expressed repentance. My pain at the hands of Richard helped me mature beyond my years. My love for the theme of surrender started in my spiritual infancy and has served me well since. I'm thankful for that man's sin against me. Time and time again, I have needed those early lessons I learned.

In *My Three Lives* I included the story of how Richard's assurance that he could help me raise money to get ministry training fell through. That too was very painful. He meant well, but the expected source for the money wasn't nearly as certain as he (and then I) thought. The Book of Job and I became very close acquaintances after that huge disappointment. But by then, I had learned to blame God and not man for such disappointments. Whatever happens, God either causes or allows it, so all spiritual battles are ultimately between us and him, not us and other humans. After that tough time, Richard and I didn't skip a beat in our relationship or fishing trips. My pain in that situation resulted in some more significant spiritual growth.

Perhaps the Ultimate Test

My final absorption of pain involving Richard was more indirect. He got fired. By that time, through his inspiration and mentoring, I was attending a ministry training school. But my parents and sister had become a part of the church where he preached. He had been used by God to do miracles in their lives also, which meant that the whole family was devastated when he was fired. I was twenty-seven years old at the time, but likely mature beyond my years—precisely because of the growth I had experienced at Richard's hands, through both extremely painful times and extremely joyful times.

When I called Richard, he handled it well, telling me to keep my eyes on Jesus and not on what men do. I called those responsible for his firing, who were friends also, and heard their side. I knew Richard well enough to know his weaknesses, and although I didn't agree with the firing, I surrendered. Richard and I stayed in touch with one another until his death several years back. He helped me handle life at its worst and best. Quite a mentor was he. Not everyone handled his firing well. My parents didn't. They switched congregations, and although they stayed involved, losing him hurt them badly. Had I been in the same congregation, it may have hurt me more than I think. Only God knows for sure.

The one thing I do know is that humans are going to disappoint and hurt us, and that includes church leaders. All pain, whether physical, emotional or spiritual, will either hinder or help, be a stumbling block or a steppingstone. We have to decide which it will be every time the pain comes our way—and come it will. Richard Hostetler brought pain and joy into my life, and I am thankful for it all. If I could rewrite my early experience in that church, it would include one of my most embarrassing moments and the utter disappointment that led me to late nights with my biblical friend Job. I would remove neither pain nor joy from that period of my spiritual development. Both were wonderful in their ultimate effects on me. So, stumbling block or steppingstone—what are your times of pain to be? Hang on to God for this brief thing we call life; you won't be sorry!

Into Heart and Life

1. Have you been hurt by someone in church leadership, and how did it affect you?

2. A repeat question from a previous chapter—do such challenges tend to become stumbling blocks or steppingstones to you? If the former, think of your painful experiences and what might have been gained from them if handled differently.

3. Think of as many times as you can when hurts led to deeper relationships and personal growth. Figure out why the pain produced positive results and how you can use those situations to help you in the present and future.

14

Journaling with God

Cast all your anxiety on him because he cares for you.
—1 Peter 5:7

In this verse, Peter gives us a command that is absolutely essential for spiritual and emotional health. But he doesn't tell us exactly how to do it. No doubt some approach comes to your mind as you read the verse, but more might be involved than would immediately register with you. This chapter describes in detail an approach that has proved invaluable to me in my decades-old walk with God. Read about it and see if it is helpful to you.

Journaling—what exactly is that? Here is the first definition found when Googling the term: "Journaling generally involves the practice of keeping a diary or journal that explores thoughts and feelings surrounding the events of your life." As you look at further online entries, you will find many emotional health experts describing the benefits of journaling. You will also find that many famous people practiced journaling as an important part of their lives. David writing his psalms would be a familiar example. So, clearly journaling is something good and perhaps very important to us humans. But as the title suggests, doing it with God is a higher level, raising something good to something great. Here I want to share examples of journaling that have blessed my life and at times helped me climb out of a deep pit spiritually and emotionally.

A Resistant Learner

My wife has journaled with God for decades, writing out her prayers daily. I resisted following her example for years, believing that I was more in touch with my emotions than she is and that prayer walks were quite sufficient to unload my burdens to God and find his solutions and direction. But eventually, my life became more complicated and the burdens overwhelming. On one memorable occasion, Theresa and I got into a spat that wasn't pretty, and it was mostly my fault (almost entirely mine, to be totally honest). It was on day one of a three-day marriage getaway. My consternation lasted long after the spat was over. She kept asking what was wrong with me, and I honestly didn't know. The next morning an extended prayer walk didn't put me in touch with what was eating at me, nor did the one the next day. I had two bad days, and I'm sure she must have had the same, having to put up with me.

The third day as we returned home, the first part of the trip was on a ferry from Nantucket to Cape Cod. For the two-plus hours on the boat, I was feverishly typing on my laptop, pouring out my pain to God. That was one intense introduction to serious journaling with God. I discovered that journaling exposed my heart and soul like nothing else. We can be full of disturbing feelings and not be able to identify them, feeling terrible and not really knowing why. Times like this occur when too many different disturbances in our personal universe are crammed in together. Praying about them or talking to others about them is helpful, for it distills them down to about the size of our mouths. Writing about them (think pen and paper) distills them down to the size of a pen point. Then the minute details emerge, and we begin to see the issues much more clearly.

That particular day, now many years ago, I discovered the main areas of my burdens. I not only listed the areas; I assigned each one a percentage of the total burden I felt. Something about getting it all written down and evaluating it started freeing me up and giving me hope. There was light at the end of the tunnel after all! As I prayed, God helped me start seeing answers to each of those five areas. My world righted itself and my wife's better husband returned! That husband discovered that his wife's approach to journaling was a hidden treasure that would bless him for years to come. It was a memorable boat ride and my introduction to journaling with God. The truth is that I am more in touch with my emotions than my wife is, and most of the time my prayer walks do accomplish what I need with God. But there are times that the victory of surrender simply will not occur without journaling with him.

The Latest Version

Let me skip to my last such victory, a very recent one. I discovered a somewhat new approach that really helped. It may help you. The year 2019 was a difficult one for me, and for us as a couple. Although our marriage is doing quite well, other aspects of life have lately been seriously challenging, to the point of me becoming overwhelmed (again). Thankfully, Theresa and I almost always remain very united in facing challenges, and we did last year as well. I won't share those challenges in any detail, but suffice it to say that I desperately needed a victory of surrender.

I started my trek in that direction by setting aside an open-ended period of time to write at my computer. After listing my burdens with which I was in touch, it became obvious that they all fit into only five categories. They were: personal concerns; family concerns; friend concerns; church concerns; and world concerns (especially those in my home country, our current society). I ended up with quite a few entries under each of these categories. Like Abraham, I had to face the truth before I could "faith" it. For the next two days, I reread what I had written and added to it. I didn't want to leave any burden hidden in the deep recesses of my heart.

On the fourth day, I highlighted everything in each category and hit the delete key. I was ready to surrender it to God, to "cast all [my] anxiety on him because he cares for [me]" (1 Peter 5:7). However, I left the category headings in place. For the next two days, I listed the most significant items under each category again that came to mind, a much smaller number than on the earlier list. Then I hit the delete button again. The next day (day six in the process), I found things to be thankful for in each of the five categories and listed them—the light at the end of the tunnel! I did the same on day seven. The following morning, I awoke with a feeling of complete peace and gratitude.

Receiving and Giving Back

Perhaps you are thinking, "Wow, Gordon, that's a long process and a lot of work!" Yes, but well worth it. You may be built differently than I am, and maybe you don't get as clogged up emotionally as I do. Good on you if that's true, in which case your journaling can follow a shorter route (as mine does most of the time). But I know people well enough to know that many are like me—worriers who want to fix everything wrong with themselves, others and the world in general. My shorter prayer list has well over 100 individuals on it and my longer one far more than that. When I add too many personal issues to those concerns for others, I can get overwhelmed, especially if I am not processing my burdens effectively and consistently, that is, almost every day. Life does tumble in, and too much of it tumbling in at once drives me to the journaling process I have just described.

Interestingly, this recent experience came at an important time. God is in control, always. We had scheduled some extended time (several days) with a couple who is very near and dear to us. They came to us at a time when they were facing a similar place in their lives that I had just worked through—that overwhelmed stage. Our first time together provided the opportunity to not only listen as they shared many of their burdens but also to share this approach, which I had just used in working through my burdens to yet another victory of surrender. Although the thought of writing down the details of painful experiences was not a positive one initially, the brother did what I recommended. I believe the writing, combined with much talking, was both cathartic and provided direction for further healing.

God is amazing—he allows us to experience hard times for at least two big reasons. One, to fight for our own spirituality and to grow though that fight. No pain, no gain. Two, to then share with others our challenges and how we found answers. We get help and we give help as a part of the one-another Christianity that the New Testament describes. For me, journaling with God is an essential part of his brand of Christianity. Although sharing my burdens with others is always an indispensable part of the process, sometimes only deep journaling with God will enable me to completely offload those burdens. I suspect the same is true for most of us. Won't you give it a try? I think you will like it!

Into Heart and Life

1. Have you ever made a gratitude list and added to it consistently? Would you write down five things for which you are grateful before going to bed—for a week or a month?

2. The next time you are troubled, start writing and try to put your feelings into written words. After doing that and exposing them to the light, pray and surrender them.

3. Seek a trusted friend (maybe your spouse) and commit to each other that you will share your journaling adventures with each other on at least three occasions.

15

PERSONAL SPIRITUAL RETREATS

Immediately Jesus made the disciples get into the boat and go on ahead of him to the other side, while he dismissed the crowd. After he had dismissed them, he went up on a mountainside by himself to pray. When evening came, he was there alone.

—Matthew 14:22-23

Becoming and remaining spiritual is a challenge. Most of us find life to be something of a roller coaster ride with its ups and downs. As my dear friend, Wyndham Shaw, used to say, "I have been up and I have been down and I will be both again!" I use many approaches to gain and maintain a reasonable level of spirituality. One of these is to embark upon personal spiritual retreats.

The idea for these came from Tom Jones and Sam Laing. Tom, then editor of DPI (Discipleship Publications International), told me that Sam had gone away by himself to a spot conducive to writing when he wrote his book *Be Still My Soul*. Tom adopted the practice when working on his books, and I decided to do the same. I have rented places with nice views for much of my writing. One of the most memorable was a little hotel in France in 1999, the spot where I wrote *The Power of Gratitude*. Writing that book only took a week, but that week was one of the highlights of my life.

More Than One Purpose

Sometimes my "retreating" is designed for writing, and at other times it is designed for personal spiritual growth or recovery. In the latter category are times that found me in challenging places spiritually. Once in Boston in early 2003, two elders' wives (Jeanie Shaw and my own wife) approached me after a leaders' meeting and said, "You need to go away by yourself and read your own book *The Victory of Surrender.*" They obviously thought I was in a bad place spiritually and needed to get my head and heart on straight again. I took their advice, going away to a secluded spot in New Hampshire, and reading three books, including VOS. As always, the time away did the job and my spiritual sanity was restored.

Several years later, after having moved from Boston to Phoenix, my wife approached me and said, "I think you are depressed, and I want you to go away by yourself and read these two books about depression." I told her that I knew something wasn't right with me spiritually and that I would ask the other elders for their advice. I sent out an email to them and I have never received answers so quickly! They agreed with my wife. I went to Sedona and stayed in a motel with a view of the beautiful red-rock mountains in that area. I read both books my wife had recommended and took extensive notes on them. I also spent a lot of time praying, as I always do on spiritual retreats. The result was that I returned home in my right mind (and spirit) once again.

My Garden of Gethsemane

A couple of years later, challenges with our ministry staff hit the overwhelming stage. I found myself humming the theme from The Twilight Zone repeatedly. I have never observed anything quite like that situation, and my need for help was obvious to everyone, including me. This time, I knew I needed a retreat of retreats, a one-of-a-kind getaway. My favorite retreat location had been at a friend's house on a small lake in New Hampshire. I called to ask if it might be available and found that it was. I booked a flight to Boston, spent time with my trusted advisor, Wyndham, enjoyed an evening with a few close friends and then made my way to New Hampshire and my retreat location.

My usual menu for spiritual nutrition consists of Bible reading, carefully selected book reading, listening to spiritual music and praying. On this occasion, I had selected several books for rereading, books that I knew had moved my heart in the past and could be expected to do the same another time. One was Exquisite Agony, by one of my favorite authors, Gene Edwards. Years earlier, my wife had been reading this book as we were en route to visit friends in Rhode Island. Obviously stirred by the book, she asked me to pull over and let her drive so that I might start reading it. I was scheduled to preach the next day, and she thought the book might influence what I would preach. Indeed it did. I changed the lesson I had planned and used some of the concepts Edwards had written about.

Interestingly, when I reread the book on my retreat, I found I had forgotten its main punchline. As Edwards discussed the serious challenges we face in life, challenges that could accurately be called our "crosses" borne for Christ, he wrote of the cross being prepared for the only sinless man ever to walk planet earth. The source of that preparation was discussed vaguely, as he asked who designed the totally undeserved suffering of Christ. As I was thinking of Satan being the designer, suddenly the book attributed the awful design to God himself, written in a way to shock the unprepared reader. Somehow the intervening years between my first reading of the book and the reading on that retreat had allowed the climax to escape my memory. I remember the shock I felt when I realized that all our crosses are in one way or another the design of God our Father.

With heart racing, I dropped the book and went outside to pray. The pieces of the puzzle, my puzzle, started falling into place. God had caused or at the least allowed my overwhelming ministry challenges to occur. Whatever happens in our lives is under his control, either directly or indirectly. Everything that takes place falls in the purview of the King of kings and Lord of lords. My cross was fashioned by my Father, just as the cross of Christ had been. That concept was then and is now a staggering one.

As I prayed, I recalled another very significant point from the book. The Garden of Gethsemane was for Jesus the night before the cross. For us, our Garden usually comes *after* we have borne our crosses. Jesus knew what was facing him before he experienced it. We only realize that our cross was designed by God in retrospect. We suffer first, filled with questions and struggles, and then we look back and see the hand of God in it all. That was my realization during that prayer time as I walked among the trees near the lake. All of a sudden, it all made sense. I wept as I thanked God for my cross. I also thanked him that my Gethsemane came in a location that reminded me of my happy childhood days, replete with forest and views of a beautiful lake. It was an experience burned into my heart and memory for all time—a Golgotha of suffering followed by a Garden of resurrection.

Reaching Another Level

These are the kinds of experiences that have made spiritual retreats rank high in my memory bank of spiritual victories. Sometimes the victories are like the one I am experiencing right now, putting my ideas into writing as I look out on a calm lake with the sun nearing the end of its visible path of today. Sometimes the victories are those of overcoming my spiritual testing and the burdens associated with it. No matter what prompts such retreats, I simply couldn't live without them. I need to escape from the hustle and bustle of life and find my own solitary places to be with my God. I may end up in a wrestling match with him, which he thankfully always wins, and at other times he and I are simply enjoying each other's company as good friends should and do. Times with him are a part of my daily routine, but on those special occasions, they are more—far more. They are spiritual retreats that take me to another level. Won't you join me?

Into Heart and Life

1. Have you ever had an overnight spiritual retreat all alone? Would you consider doing it, especially when you are facing a big spiritual challenge or when you recognize that your faith has become weak? Make a plan.

2. In longer quiet times, do you listen to spiritual music while you read, write or pray? If not, will you try using such music to build you up spiritually? Getting the lyrics online and reading them as you listen can really enhance the experience.

3. Have you encouraged others to go on this type of spiritual retreat, including your mate if you are married? Will you?

16

I Want to Know Christ

I want to know Christ—yes, to know the power of his resurrection and participation in his sufferings, becoming like him in his death, and so, somehow, attaining to the resurrectiona from the dead.

—Philippians 3:10-11

Anyone who has read much of my writing figures out that I have struggled with my view of God and how I think he views me. One part of that battle traces back to being raised in a very legalistic church setting. That is easy to understand on an intellectual basis, although accepting the needed solutions is still at times an emotional challenge. The other part of my struggle has been both intellectual and emotional. This means, in simple terms, that I haven't fully figured out how to harmonize my view of God in the Old Testament with my view of Jesus in the New. While I reject the heretic Marcion's view from the early second century, a view that essentially saw the God of the Old Testament as inferior to the God of the New Testament, I at least understand how he could come to that position, even though the two-God theory was and is heresy. But as you will see, this harmonization is a bigger issue than many realize. The answers in this chapter help to satisfy me and thus help me intellectually and emotionally. I hope they do the same for you.

Knowing Christ was Paul's number one goal in life. His goal was not to accomplish great things, although he was in a class by himself in that regard. His goal was not to avoid pain and enjoy a carefree life. He simply wanted to know Christ to the fullest extent possible. To me, his loftiest passage explaining this desire is Philippians 3:7–14. I suggest you stop and read it, slowly and carefully. In verse 8, Paul says that he considers everything a loss compared to the surpassing greatness of knowing Christ. In verse 10, he explains in several stunning phrases the depths of his pursuit of knowing Christ: "I want to know Christ—yes, to know the power of his resurrection and participation in his sufferings, becoming like him in his death." No other goal or desire in his life could compare to this endeavor.

My Challenge

My biggest challenge in relating to God is a long-standing one. I have studied the Old Testament a lot from my earliest days of studying the Bible seriously. At age twenty-seven I gave up my career in music as a band director and professional musician, and enrolled in a ministry training program called a school of preaching. That program was aimed at in-depth study of the biblical text, and the Old Testament was a primary focus. We went through every one of those thirty-nine books in a verse-by-verse fashion. The God described therein (as I saw him) was scary. It was easier to see him as the King and the Judge than as the Father and Friend. A few people, like Abraham and David, might have ascended high enough to become friends of God, but such people seemed to be few and far between in the pages of what comprises the bulk of the Bible (more than two-thirds by word count).

I think back to reaching out to our neighbors across the street from us in Phoenix. This retired couple started their spiritual journey by attending what we called "Chicken Sunday," a bring-your-neighbor day when chicken was the entrée for the lunch after services. Our neighbors loved the food and the fellowship and consented to start studying the Bible with us. Although I didn't give them this direction, George started doing a lot of reading in the Old Testament. One day when I went over to study with him, he sat on the sofa looking rather staggered emotionally. He had experienced much the same reaction to the Old Testament as I had, and it almost scared him into stopping the studies. I encouraged him to focus on Jesus and the New Testament, which he did. Both he and his wife ended up getting baptized, but that early study of the Old Testament was unquestionably a bump in his road to salvation.

No Simplistic Answer

Although my recommendation was the right advice, I knew enough about the Bible to know that this counsel was not simplistic. Christ is Deity and as much a part of those OT scary events as is the Father. As Hebrews 13:8 puts it: "Jesus Christ is the same yesterday and today and forever." God's nature never changes. It can't. In calling the Corinthians to be obedient and avoid sin, Paul used an example of God's judgment upon Israel during their wilderness wandering era. He was very explicit in showing that Christ was totally involved in that terrifying judgment. Read it.

> For I do not want you to be ignorant of the fact, brothers and sisters, that our ancestors were all under the cloud and that they all passed through the sea. They were all baptized into Moses in the cloud and in the sea. They all ate the same spiritual food and drank the same spiritual drink; for they drank from the spiritual rock that accompanied them, and that rock was Christ. Nevertheless, God was not pleased with most of them; their bodies were scattered in the wilderness.
>
> Now these things occurred as examples to keep us from setting our hearts on evil things as they did. Do not be idolaters, as some of them were; as it is written: "The people sat down to eat and drink and got up to indulge in revelry." We should not commit sexual immorality, as some of them did—and in one day twenty-three thousand of them died. We should not test Christ, as some

of them did—and were killed by snakes. And do not grumble, as some of them did—and were killed by the destroying angel.

These things happened to them as examples and were written down as warnings for us, on whom the culmination of the ages has come. So, if you think you are standing firm, be careful that you don't fall! (1 Corinthians 10:1-12)

The Old Testament is replete with such descriptions of God's judgment, and many of them are indeed terrifying. Seeing God as Father and Friend is not an easy thing to do, but our Jesus who hung upon a cross for us cannot be separated from what we read in the Old Testament. In fact, he is described by Isaiah as "Mighty God" and "Everlasting Father" just as surely as he is called "Wonderful Counselor" and "Prince of Peace" (Isaiah 9:6). There can be no doubt that in this context, the one we call Jesus is being described in prophecy.

Help Me, Please!

What are we to do with all of this? Please help me, you might be saying, if you are built like me emotionally. These concepts are biblical, and they are very serious and likely disturbing. Right? Many things could be mentioned as possible approaches to help with what seems a real dilemma, but I will focus on two.

First, I think it is almost impossible for us to grasp what living in four hundred years of slavery and sin had done to Israel. Their knowledge of God was virtually nil when Moses was sent to deliver them. They were about as far from God as possible. To say that God had to deal with them as children is a woefully inadequate way of describing them. They were more like sin-hardened adults who had a hugely difficult time grasping spiritual concepts, much less following them.

When we read their history, we are puzzled to discover their rebellions, which often came right after being blessed incredibly with miracles and daily reminders of the presence of God among them. These reminders did not require faith either, for they were in plain sight. They could see God's presence in the ten plagues in Egypt and the parting of the Red Sea in their exodus. They saw it in the ever-present pillar of fire by night and pillar of cloud by day that guided them from place to place. They could see it in the manna, quail and water being provided miraculously for their food. They could see it even in hearing his voice and experiencing the earthquakes they knew were of him. Yet, these manifestations of God's presence, miracles and blessings appeared to have no lasting effect on them.

Things changed little after the nation settled in the promised land. Rebellion was the order of the day for centuries. Yes, at times the nation repented and was blessed by God when he removed the hand of judgment from them for a while. But the Book of Judges shows the same cycle over and over and over again: sin, judgment, repentance, blessings; sin, judgment, repentance, sin. That cycle describes Israel's entire history perfectly.

The Bottom-Line Problem

Goodness gracious! What was wrong with those people anyway? How could they have seen such evidence of God and continued in that deadly cycle for hundreds of years? Were they simply the most depraved population to ever inhabit the earth? No, they were simply humans—just like us; humans without Jesus on a cross. And therein lies the answer. Jesus wasn't wrong when he said this: "Apart from me you can do nothing" (John 15:5). The "somethings" good that humans do without him today are the same as the "somethings" good that the Israelite nation did at certain points in the cycle described above. The good could not last; it was destined to fail. Take a good look at our world right now. Do we really need examples from the Old Testament to show the depravity of humankind without a crucified Savior?

Once, I was able to study with a group of graduate students from China who were at San Diego State University for a high-level math course. After their course was over, they went back to China. I had two or three nights to share Christ with that group of about fifteen male students. My introduction had to be simple, since they were atheists and devoid of any religious training.

I said something to this effect to begin: "All religions have this in common: they all tell you to be good and to do good. Christianity is the one singular religion that starts off by telling you that you cannot be good and do good. It is humanly impossible." From there, I went on to explain that only with God's help could we do good and be good, but that his help could only accomplish that in the form of a cross. This path to the cross took centuries to develop, and the goal of it could only be achieved in one way. Our Creator had to become human and die for humans. No other reality could provide the means and the motivation to change us and keep us changed for a lifetime. History has demonstrated that fact since the dawn of the human race.

What Then?

Second, we are now ready to move on toward finding a satisfying answer to knowing God. Prior to Jesus, the God/Man, dying on a cross, humanity always became so depraved that God had to restrain them in the only way that could work in the midst of rebellion—judgment. These judgments were applied in direct proportion to the depth of the depravity present. The story of humanity without God on a cross has always been the same, starting with Cain, who "raised Cain" by killing his own brother; continuing with a depravity of earth's inhabitants described as "every inclination of the thoughts of the human heart was only evil all the time" (Genesis 6:5); continuing with the sordid, rebellious history of Israel; continuing further with the descent of the non-Jewish world into the hellish state described in Romans 1:18–32; and continuing to this very moment of a world steeped in sin and becoming more depraved with every passing day. Is that not enough evidence to convince any rational person that only one answer is available?

I Must Know Jesus

Paul said that he wanted to know Jesus because he understood that he must know Jesus in order to escape the whirlpool of sinful humanity. There are no other answers. As the hymn puts it, "There's no other way to be happy in Jesus, but to trust and obey." This singular answer is made clear by verses like these:

John 1:14

The Word became flesh and made his dwelling among us. We have seen his glory, the glory of the one and only Son, who came from the Father, full of grace and truth.

John 14:5-9

Thomas said to him, "Lord, we don't know where you are going, so how can we know the way?"

Jesus answered, "I am the way and the truth and the life. No one comes to the Father except through me. If you really know me, you will know my Father as well. From now on, you do know him and have seen him."

Philip said, "Lord, show us the Father and that will be enough for us."

Jesus answered: "Don't you know me, Philip, even after I have been among you such a long time? Anyone who has seen me has seen the Father. How can you say, 'Show us the Father'?"

Colossians 2:9-10

For in Christ all the fullness of the Deity lives in bodily form, and in Christ you have been brought to fullness. He is the head over every power and authority.

Is Seeing Believing?

Those first apostles had a difficult time believing Jesus was who he said he was, even after seeing him. It seems that we humans today often have the same problem. Through the pages of the

New Testament, Jesus is revealed; and through the lives of those who follow him, he is revealed as well. Just as surely as he was in his fullness the demonstration of God in the flesh, his family, the church, is in Christ's fullness the demonstration of him in the flesh (our flesh). So yes, we can see God in the person of Christ, and the world can see Jesus in the persons of Christ. But the better each of us knows Christ, the better we will demonstrate him. Thus, we too must be able to say sincerely, "I want to know Christ," and then pursue what can enable us to know him as fully as possible. Knowing about him is not the goal; it is to know him through a personal relationship with him. Just how can we seek such as a lifetime endeavor?

Tying the Two Ends Together

The two ends to which I refer are being able to harmonize what we see of God in the Old Testament and what we see of him through Jesus in the New Testament. Taking a deeper look at the depraved nature of man throughout all of history helps me understand that God's judgments, while seeming harsh, are not. They were what was absolutely necessary to keep humankind from destroying itself. They were what was necessary to keep the nation of Israel within shouting distance of the spiritual concepts necessary to pave the way for the coming of the Messiah. God's judgment was fashioned to fit the depravity of humans; it was always exactly what was needed—no more and no less. God doesn't make mistakes, for he cannot make mistakes. Whatever he has ever done to and with the humanity he created is always right, whether we understand it or not. As Paul said in Romans 3:4, "Let God be true and every human being a liar." We creatures simply must humble out and stop questioning the Creator, who is always good and forever will be.

Now we are in a place to start seeing and knowing Jesus. The Old Testament introduced him through prophecies about him and his coming into our world. The New Testament reveals all about him that we need to know and love him and follow him. Here is a passage that has helped me lately, a lot:

At that time Jesus said, "I praise you, Father, Lord of heaven and earth, because you have hidden these things from the wise and learned, and revealed them to little children. Yes, Father, for this is what you were pleased to do.

"All things have been committed to me by my Father. No one knows the Son except the Father, and no one knows the Father except the Son and those to whom the Son chooses to reveal him.

"Come to me, all you who are weary and burdened, and I will give you rest. Take my yoke upon you and learn from me, for I am gentle and humble in heart, and you will find rest for your souls. For my yoke is easy and my burden is light." (Matthew 11:25-30)

Digging Deeper

Let's dig into a passage that introduces a Jesus who still may be rather a stranger to many, even to professed believers. First, we must become like little children if we are to know the real Jesus. In fact, he said that unless we do become like children, we cannot enter the kingdom of heaven (Matthew 18:3). One of my favorite psalms is Psalm 131, which describes what happens when our humility and trust in God is like the trust of a child with its mother. "But I have calmed and quieted myself, I am like a weaned child with its mother; like a weaned child I am content" (Psalm 131:2).

In Matthew 11:27, Jesus goes on to say that he can be known only when the Father reveals him to us, and the Father can be known only when Jesus reveals him to us. Besides becoming like little children, what else are we to do? In verse 28, he says that we must come to him, but the prerequisites for coming to him include being weary and burdened and desiring rest for our souls. You may be thinking that you don't like to be weary and burdened. Neither do I. However, that is the ongoing path to knowing Jesus. Life was not designed to be a life of ease and carefree happiness; it was designed to make us more and more like Jesus and prepare us for heaven. If we don't stay in touch with our sinfulness and need for him, we will not keep coming to him. We will go to the world to seek our fulfillment. God knows the strength of that temptation we face every day, and the more we have materially, the stronger the temptation to go in that direction. True rest, that which brings rest in our very souls, is connected to ongoing repentance and surrender, resulting in being refreshed (Acts 3:19).

The Bombshell

The bombshell in this passage is Jesus' statement in verse 29. First, he tenderly says that we must take his yoke upon us as we follow him and keep learning from him. Then comes the kicker: he is gentle and humble in heart. Be sure to get this point: Jesus didn't become humble when he became a man; he became a man because he was already humble. All the different views we seem to be getting of God all through the Bible cannot be understood without understanding that he is in his very nature gentle and humble. Those seemingly harsh judgments we have been discussing do not and cannot change his nature. He has always been gentle and humble and will remain so forever.

What a lover of our souls he must be, to come down as a man and put up with depraved mankind as he was despised and rejected by them (Isaiah 53) to the very end, and finally nailed to the cross. And from the cross, what was foremost on his heart? "Father, forgive them" (Luke 23:34). Yes, he is gentle and humble first, last and always. He could not be otherwise, for that is who God is. No wonder he hates pride in us; it is ungodlike to the nth degree.

Now It All Fits!

It does all fit together, at least to me and hopefully to you. God's judgments are always based on what is best for us individually and collectively. He is never harsh, for he only does what sin necessitates being done. Ultimately, the just penalty for sin had to be paid, and it could only be paid in one way, so he came down and paid that awful price personally. What a God is he! On the cross, he paid a debt that he did not owe so that we would no longer owe a debt that we could not pay. On the cross, he was treated in harsh and unrelenting terms so that we might be treated as if we had never sinned. And that is what this legal term means in Greek: *justified*—just-as-if-I'd never sinned.

I hope we understand better the God of the Old Testament, by whatever names he has given himself. In the New Testament, his name is Jesus. He has always been gentle and humble in heart, and this he will forever remain. Fears of him alleviated, we see him for who he is and not as Satan tries to depict him. Do you not want to know a Jesus like that? Is following him on his terms a burden? Are the challenges that he sends or allows to come into our lives bigger than the rest for our souls that he promises? In John 15:15, he made it clear that he would much rather be friends with us than simply our Master. Relax and enjoy his gentle, humble friendship. With Paul, let us say: "I want to know Christ—yes, to know the power of his resurrection and participation in his sufferings, becoming like him in his death."

Into Heart and Life

1. Did anything in this chapter reach out and "grab" you? If yes, what was it and why do you think it resonated with you? (Perhaps there were several things—if so, you should write them out, along with why you think they did, and then do more praying and contemplating about them.)

2. Do you tend to view God in the Old Testament differently than you view Jesus? If yes, how and why?

3. When you think of God, do you picture him more as a King and Judge than as a Father and Friend? If yes, think and pray more about Jesus being humble and gentle and look for passages in the New Testament that demonstrate those qualities in him.

17

Happy New Year – Through Repentance

"Repent, then, and turn to God, so that your sins may be wiped out, that times of refreshing may come from the Lord."

—Acts 3:19

As I write this, we have entered the year 2020 and this is the third day of it. Good. I'm glad to put 2019 behind me. It has been a very difficult year for me. It started out with a knee replacement surgery that was both painful and scary, the scary part caused by much loss of blood after coming home the same day after the surgery. Add to that the fact that my pain is still just about as bad as before the surgery nearly a year later. So not a good beginning to the year.

Death, Death and More Death

Skipping over many other trying events, we come to the death in June of Theresa's older brother, Barney, the first of our siblings to go. That marked the end of one era and the beginning of another, an unwelcome grief to say the least. I had known Barney for about sixty years and been his brother-in-law for almost fifty-five. Then came the sudden and unexpected death of Bob Gempel in August. Bob was a fellow elder in the early part of our Boston years, one with whom I enjoyed sweet fellowship as a dear friend along with working side by side in our church roles.

November 21 was that fateful day on which I lost my best friend, Wyndham. I was happy for him to escape the ravages of his cruel disease and enter into his eternal reward, but struck deeply with my personal loss and the loss felt by his family and so many others. The grief of this death, along with the two others, all within a six-month period, took a toll on me emotionally and spiritually. I cry as I write this. Grief doesn't let go easily nor quickly.

During these same months, I was trying to edit and write additional chapters for a second edition of *The Power of Gratitude,* but ended up writing this new book instead. Just as 2020 began, I realized what a low place I had been in for some months, a realization that had eluded me because I always tend to just keep on keeping on in good times and bad. That is a positive path to take in many ways, but it can deceive you into thinking you are doing better than you really are. That was certainly true of me.

Practice What You Preach (or Write)

In another chapter I wrote about having personal spiritual retreats. When the reality of where I was at hit home, my first thought was that I needed to go on one of those spiritual getaways I had recently written about but hadn't done in several years. I decided to go on a retreat and to reread my book *The Victory of Surrender,* as I always do on these retreats, along with a couple of other books I usually reread on such occasions. It seemed a good plan to help me re-surrender, get out of the doldrums and start the new year well.

The next day I began reading Tom and Sheila Jones' book *To Live Is Christ,* a devotional book based on the Apostle Paul's letter to the Philippians. Every member of the Dallas-Fort Worth church, my home church, was given the book and asked to read it as a daily devotional guide to begin the new year. As I read and thought about Philippians, the light bulbs started going off. A need to simply surrender in adverse circumstances wasn't my real need. What I really needed was repentance. Here are the passages that really touched my heart:

Philippians 2:3-5

Do nothing out of selfish ambition or vain conceit. Rather, in humility value others above yourselves, not looking to your own interests but each of you to the interests of the others. In your relationships with one another, have the same mindset as Christ Jesus.

Philippians 2:14-15

Do everything without grumbling or arguing, so that you may become blameless and pure, "children of God without fault in a warped and crooked generation." Then you will shine among them like stars in the sky.

Philippians 3:13-14

Brothers and sisters, I do not consider myself yet to have taken hold of it. But one thing I do: Forgetting what is behind and straining toward what is ahead, I press on toward the goal to win the prize for which God has called me heavenward in Christ Jesus.

Philippians 4:4-7

Rejoice in the Lord always. I will say it again: Rejoice! Let your gentleness be evident to all. The Lord is near. Do not be anxious about anything, but in every situation, by prayer and petition, with thanksgiving, present your requests to God. And the peace of God, which transcends all understanding, will guard your hearts and your minds in Christ Jesus.

The Real Bottom Line

I have said for many years that my biggest root sins are selfishness and pride. I realized that my current issue was mostly due to just plain selfishness. I have been struggling with impatience and anger, mainly because I wasn't dealing with my challenges spiritually. My selfish self wants the world to revolve around his desires and preferences. I know anger can result from personal hurts like grief, but I think most of mine results from selfishness. I haven't had a servant's heart although I have not quit serving in many ways. Bottom line, I just don't like denying self. I have allowed myself to become negative and critical, which means that I haven't been denying self and simply obeying what God says.

Paul's inspired admonitions in the above passages are not suggestions; they are commands. My unspiritual attitudes are not from an unsurrendered heart nearly as much as they are from a non–self-denied heart. In its very essence, it is a refusal to repent and a willingness to let circumstances and self-interest shape my viewpoints; to let emotions rule rather than Christ. I just needed to humble out and repent and then start doing what Jesus gave as the first step in being a disciple: deny self, count others better than myself, serve and rejoice—all of which things are purely a matter of obedience. I have been disobeying and blaming it on circumstances, but circumstances are not my root problem. Repentance of selfishness and pride are my deeper issues, as always.

The answers I needed are quite clear and quite simple, although not easy: denying self, taking up my cross daily (accepting the hard times with faith) and following (imitating) Jesus. Obedience to my Creator, who wrote the Manual of life, will make life work according to his plan. I am so relieved! I see my problem and I see the answer and by God's grace I can do it—just repent! It may be easier to get psychological in explaining emotions and behavior, but it often is far better to identify our sins and deal with them according to God's prescription. Yes, there are times when emotional issues call for counseling and perhaps professional help, but this is not one of those times for me. Otherwise, I wouldn't feel so refreshed by repenting!

I'm reminded of the newly married sister, who after sitting with Theresa and me for hours in a marriage counseling session with her and her husband, finally said this: "It's almost midnight. Can't you just tell us what sins have caused our marriage problems and call us to repent so we can all go to bed?!" Wow! The woman was right, and I promptly did exactly what she requested. Now I'm applying her advice to myself—once again. No wonder I feel so refreshed going into the new year. Repentance brings refreshment (Acts 3:19). Praise Jesus! Happy New Year!

Into Heart and Life

1. How can you tell the difference between psychological emotional issues and sin issues?

2. How does your selfishness show itself?

3. What does repentance mean to you, and what do you most need to repent of right now?

18

My Hope Is in Our Youth

The proverbs of Solomon son of David, king of Israel:
for gaining wisdom and instruction;
   for understanding words of insight;
for receiving instruction in prudent behavior,
   doing what is right and just and fair;
for giving prudence to those who are simple,
   knowledge and discretion to the young—
let the wise listen and add to their learning,
   and let the discerning get guidance.

—Proverbs 1:1-5

I am very thankful for the youth of our churches. My hope for the future of our churches is in them. While I appreciate all that God has been able to use me and others of the older generations to accomplish, my hope for what lies ahead is not in us. We have done our thing, and now the future is up to our younger generations. Many in my generation have a difficult time recognizing this and thus have a difficult time letting go of the reins. But God and time will see to it that we do, you can trust that! My own rapidly increasing attendance at memorial services makes the point, loudly! It would be far better if we were to recognize the need and have a planned generational transition much sooner than later.

That is my prayer and my plea in this chapter.

A Lost Generation

Our family of churches, the ICOC, has been seriously affected in negative ways by losing a generation of leaders. In the early years of this millennium, we suffered as a movement a serious upheaval and a series of reactions. While we needed something to jar us into a realization of ineffective and wrongful spiritual building in our serious attempts to carry out the Great Commission, we experienced more damage than we realized at the time. A grave part of the damage was the loss of a generation of leaders (and members). As our overall membership declined, our available funds to support ministry staff declined. Young ministry staff leaders in their twenties were laid off because of these dwindling contributions and the decision to direct available funds toward ministry staff who were older and dependent on those funds for supporting themselves and their families in their career choice.

It took some years to start recovering and raising up younger leaders again in significant numbers, but by then we had another problem. Leadership roles were limited, and although we were adding young people to our ministry staffs, their opportunities for advancement into more influential roles were already filled by older staff members. The young ones could lead campus ministries or youth programs or in some cases, small churches. But the opportunities to lead in roles that carried with them a voice that was heard on a broader scale simply weren't there. When we were growing fast in the 1980s and 1990s, leadership advancement was a natural part of our growth. When growth stopped, suddenly the whole picture was different, and natural progressions in leadership were stymied.

The result has been that older, established leaders have guided most of the directions we have taken as a whole. The same older crowd is leading in the same older ways, and those ways have ceased to produce the results they once did. Without younger leaders with younger thinking whose voices are not just heard, but allowed to shape our future directions, we will continue down the path of diminishing growth and relevance with the upcoming generations. As I put it bluntly from time to time, many (not all) of those who were once new wine breaking old wineskins have themselves become old wineskins—and don't realize it. It pains me to say such things, but facts are facts, and I think these are indisputable and need to be recognized, admitted and acted upon.

Since our growth rate is diminishing, the natural progression of having more and more younger leaders entering the fray is not going to happen organically. We older leaders are going to have to find alternative roles for ourselves, like shepherding and teaching (teaching was my choice over a decade ago), and put younger leaders in roles that allow them to help us figure out how to turn the growth rate around. That might sound radical, but I hope it also sounds rational, because I believe it is the only rational choice available. The lost generation syndrome can be reversed, but only if we are willing to make radical choices that seem unnatural to us.

Youth and Radical Change

Christianity had its beginning with youth, for they are the ones open to entertaining new ideas and approaches. The apostles were likely quite young. If John the apostle wrote his five documents (his Gospel, his three letters and Revelation) when tradition says he did, he must have been a teenager when called to be an apostle. I suspect most of the other apostles were also young. History shows that radical things done in the spiritual realm are almost always initiated by youth. Youth and radical go together, not old and radical. It is the nature of aging to become tradition bound, and the recognition and rejection of traditions becomes more and more an elusive task. I wish it weren't so, but it is, and that is why my hope is in the youth among us.

As that exciting first century church aged, it moved further and further away from the truth and replaced it with traditions. Thankfully, the Holy Spirit predicted this departure through Paul in no uncertain terms. Passages like 1 Timothy 4:1-3 and 2

Timothy 4:2–4 demonstrate that God didn't want this turning aside to take later generations by surprise. They also serve as a warning about how easy it is to move from truth to traditions, an ever-present danger in every age. Further, the danger is not just limited to traditions that directly violate Scripture; the ones that are not unbiblical but become ineffective are in some ways more damaging, since they block the effective spreading of the gospel. That type represents our current challenge, for said simply, we as a movement are stuck.

As history unfolded, it was only a matter of time before some youthful radicals had enough of the Establishment's traditions and drew a line in the sand. Well, in this case, it was actually a document nailed to a door. Martin Luther nailed his "Ninety-Five Theses" against Catholic teachings to the church door in Wittenberg, Germany. He was in his early thirties when this momentous event took place, but he was much younger when his radicalness was taking shape. Another very important figure in the Protestant Reformation was John Calvin, who began his extensive writings when yet in his twenties. Once again, history connects the terms "youth," "radical" and "change."

Then we come to the Age of Reason, when the American Restoration Movement was born. Much about the Reformation was commendable; much about its effectiveness was not so commendable. By 1700, there were 150 divisions within Protestantism. In the early 1800s, leaders from various denominations started questioning the concept of reformation. Trying to reform something with so many divergences from the Bible was proving to be impossible in the quest for religious unity. Thus the idea of just going back to the New Testament as the pattern for Christianity and restoring it gained ground quickly. The two most influential leaders started their quest for restoration of the NT church when they were still young. Alexander Campbell was in his twenties and Barton W. Stone was just about thirty.

Fast forward to the origins of my current church association, now known as the International Churches of Christ. This group began as a spiritual renewal group within what I now call the Mainline Churches of Christ. It was at the outset a campus ministry movement in the 1970s. Its epicenter was in Gainesville, Florida at the Crossroads Church of Christ, and it was spearheaded by Chuck Lucas when he was about thirty and later pushed forward by Kip McKean when he was about twenty-five. That Crossroads Movement became the Discipling Movement and the Boston Movement and ultimately the ICOC as we now know it.

The Future – Scary and Exciting!

Is not the pattern of radical spiritual change fairly obvious? Doesn't it always start with radical youth who burn with a desire to change the world? That is why I am so thankful for the youth among us. They must pick up the baton and do what we are currently failing to do—affect the whole world significantly with the rapid spread of the gospel. Christianity has never been about having a nice, comfortable church to make us feel warm inside once or twice a week. It was designed by its Designer to radically affect the world.

Our society is changing so fast that keeping up with how people think is almost impossible for us older folks. We don't understand youth and they don't understand us too well either. We use similar words but often are speaking a different language. But that is nothing new. It has always been that way. Generation gaps are real, and really important to at least recognize (not just decry). I highly recommend reading Chapter 21 in Michael Burns' book *All Things to All People.* The title of that chapter is "World War Z," and I can promise you that it is one of the most eye-opening, disturbing pieces we of the older generation could read. It is for those of all generations among us a must-read—so please read it!

Youth—Christ's mission now depends on you! Grab hold of it and GO! People like me who have done their best want to see our work as only a foundation of what you can do as you build to the sky with the help of Almighty God. I am praying for you and already thanking God for what you are going to do. I am also praying for us older ones, that we will help you begin doing it—now. Let's all please do our part, and may God lead us to do it soon!

Into Heart and Life

1. What in this chapter struck you the most positively? The most negatively? Think through the reasons for each.

2. If you are older, how can you best encourage the younger people in the church; if you are younger, how can you best encourage the older ones in the church?

3. How comfortable are you with the concept of "radical" change, and what does the example of Jesus and the early church teach you about such?

Books by Gordon Ferguson

All available at www.ipibooks.com